Praise for *Dragged Off*

"Dr. David Anh Dao's memoir *Dragged Off: Refusing to Give Up My Seat on the Way to the American Dream* is a study in resilience and determination. From his escape of the collapsing South Vietnamese city of Saigon at the end of the war, to his early days studying medicine in America, to his struggle to regain his medical license and good name, Dr. Dao shows the grit and stubbornness necessary to make the American dream come true. His refusal to give up his seat on a United Airlines flight, and the ensuing assault he suffered, is emblematic of how far we, the people, still have to travel to create a world with liberty and justice for all. Told with grace and dign̶ ̶t̶h̶i̶s̶ ̶i̶s̶ ̶a̶ ̶b̶o̶o̶k̶ ̶y̶o̶u̶ ̶w̶o̶n̶'̶t̶ ̶w̶a̶n̶t̶ ̶t̶o̶ put down."

— ̶ ̶ ̶ ̶ ̶ ̶ ̶ ̶ ̶ ̶ iz̶ed scholar and speaker and auth̶

' ̶ ̶ ̶ ̶ ̶ ̶ ̶ ̶ being dragged off a United Airlines flight in 2017, but Dr. David Anh Dao's story is much more interesting than those fifteen minutes of fame would imply. *Dragged Off: Refusing to Give Up My Seat on the Way to the American Dream* is no ordinary immigrant's tale. Dr. David Anh Dao's escape from Saigon during its fall to the North Vietnamese in 1975 on a crowded boat full of refugees heading for an uncertain future in America is just one step on his amazing journey. Dao shows how to rise and fall and rise again even higher in this memoir, which will become an inspiration, and perhaps a cautionary tale for all who read it. Dao delves deeply into the cost of the American dream and makes it seem achievable, no matter the price tag."

—MJ Fievre, author of *Empowered Black Girl*

DRAGGED OFF

DRAGGED OFF

Refusing to Give Up My Seat
on the Way to the American Dream

DR. DAVID ANH DAO

mango
PUBLISHING

CORAL GABLES

Cover Design: Roberto Núñez
Cover illustration: Sergey at Logan Masterworks
Layout & Design: Roberto Núñez

For permission requests, please contact the publisher at:
Mango Publishing Group
2850 S Douglas Road, 2nd Floor
Coral Gables, FL 33134 USA
info@mango.bz

For special orders, quantity sales, course adoptions and corporate sales, please email the publisher at sales@mango.bz. For trade and wholesale sales, please contact Ingram Publisher Services at customer.service@ingramcontent.com or +1.800.509.4887.

Dragged Off: Refusing to Give Up My Seat on the Way to the American Dream

Library of Congress Cataloging-in-Publication number: 2020951504
ISBN: (print) 978-1-64250-401-9, (ebook) 978-1-64250-402-6
BISAC category code: POL004000, POLITICAL SCIENCE / Civil Rights

Printed in the United States of America

Chapter One

I was sixty-nine years old when I was forcibly removed from a United Airlines flight. There's a good chance that the United Airlines incident is the only thing you know about me. And there's a good chance you saw that infamous video before I did.

I remember what happened on the plane. I remember being asked to leave. I remember refusing. I remember being removed by force. At some point, I lost consciousness. I don't remember how I got to the hospital.

I woke up to find that I was suffering from a concussion, as well as a broken nose and several broken teeth. I had a suture in my mouth. My daughter Crystal was in the room with me. Before I could tell her what had happened to me, she was urging me to do two things: get a lawyer and refrain, under any circumstances, from turning on the television.

Hiring a lawyer made sense. I knew that the security team had crossed a line in how they'd handled the situation. I also knew from a lifetime of experience that, if I didn't call them out on what they'd done, they'd do the same thing to other passengers in the future.

But why did my daughter urge me not to turn on the television? And why had she taken my phone away from me? Clearly, she didn't want me to get upset while I was in the hospital. My imagination immediately began running through possibilities. Something had happened since I'd lost consciousness. Had there been some natural disaster? A terrorist attack? What didn't she want me to know? Even though I promised that I wouldn't turn on the television, as soon as I was alone in my room, that's what I did. It didn't take long for me to find a channel running the story that she didn't want me to see.

Of course, the news story that she hadn't wanted me to see was my own. The incident had occurred only hours earlier, yet the video had already gone viral on a global scale. People all over the world had seen what had happened to me. More importantly, people all over the world had *condemned* what had happened to me.

Far from upsetting me, this global show of outrage and support touched me deeply. It confirmed that millions of people shared the same ideal that I've held all my life: the belief that everybody has rights. Nobody deserves to be treated the way I'd been treated on that plane. I cried as I flipped through the channels, listening to different newscasters express their shock over what had happened.

I'm sure that most of the people reading this story will assume that April 9, 2017, was the worst day of my life. But it wasn't. In 1970, I was forced to leave the National Conservatory for Vietnamese Traditional Music. In 1975, I had to flee Vietnam (leaving my parents and siblings behind) after the fall of Saigon. In 1977, I was attacked while working as a physician in the Indiana State Prison. In 2003, my office manager robbed my business of thousands of dollars. In 2004, I had to give up my medical license. And in 2005, I was convicted of a crime I didn't commit.

And yet, looking back on the last seventy years of my life, what I feel more than anything else is a profound sense of gratitude over my good fortune. I have been blessed with an amazing life, and I want to spend whatever years I have left helping others who haven't been as fortunate as I have.

After the United Airlines incident, the media reported various bits and pieces of my life, painting a distorted picture. At one point, several sources even confused me with a different Dr. David Dao.

I'm writing this story to set the record straight, but also to give some insight into why I didn't simply give up my seat when I was asked (which I'm sure many people wondered).

My story begins over fifty years ago in Vietnam.

Chapter Two

I was born in Vietnam and raised in a large family with six brothers and sisters. My mother didn't have time for a job since she was raising seven children. That meant my father had to support our family with his job as a nurse. As anyone who's raised a family knows, you take the opportunities you're offered when it comes to making more money, so when my father was offered the chance to train for a better career in the army, the fact that his studies would relocate him to the United States for several months didn't deter him. While he was away, our family stayed with a friend of my mother's.

When my father returned, he became convinced that my mother had been having an affair while he was away. I never saw any evidence that my mother had cheated on my father, and, to my knowledge, none of my siblings ever saw anything either. To this day, I don't know what put that idea in my father's head, but he couldn't be convinced otherwise. Eventually, his questioning of my mother went from simple accusations to outright abuse.

One day, I came home from school to find my mother tied to a bed. Her hair had been cut. As I untied her, she told me that my father had done this to her. He'd left her tied to the bed when he went to work. I knew if she was still here when he got home, chances were good that he would kill her. So I told her to leave—to run away to someplace where she'd be safe.

When my father returned home, he was furious that I'd let my mother go and began slapping me, demanding to know where she'd gone. Since she hadn't told me, there was no way I could have told him even if I'd wanted to. Eventually, my father decided that the only way he would be able to find my mother would be to file a lawsuit against her, at which point the court would have to track her down so she could appear at the trial.

I should point out that attitudes toward marital infidelity were quite different in Vietnam than they were in the United States. While cheating on your spouse in 1960s America certainly carried a stigma, the same behavior was a crime in Vietnam. So my father was able to file a lawsuit against my mother on the charge of infidelity. He was even considered well within his rights to question her the way he did. Despite having no evidence, no eyewitness testimony, and no confession, my mother was found guilty of marital infidelity and sentenced to six months in jail. I chose not to attend the trial and was told about the verdict when my father got home.

While my mother was in jail, my father filed for a divorce. Given how infidelity was handled, it won't surprise you to know that divorce was also looked down upon in 1960s Vietnam. Not only did it reflect badly on my mother and father, but my siblings and I were also treated differently because of the divorce. In many ways, being the child of a divorced couple was similar to being the child of a criminal (which, I suppose, I was as well). People not only assumed my parents were somehow immoral or untrustworthy, but they also assumed that whatever was "wrong" with them had somehow transferred to their children. I didn't experience overt name-calling or accusations, but something more subtle: Once they knew about my parents, people looked at me differently and seemed more on guard around me.

After my mother was released from jail, she didn't stop by our house because my father had threatened to kill her if he ever saw her again. One of my cousins told me where she was staying, but I wasn't allowed to visit her there. I know that she started a sewing business in ChoLon (a city near Saigon) and never remarried, but otherwise we lost touch with one another. My father raised us on his own after the divorce, but I was already near the age when I had to plan for my own career.

Probably the most significant reason that I first pursued a career in medicine was to bring some honor back to my family. Being a doctor in Vietnam brought with it a level of prestige, as it does in most parts of the world. As a doctor, not only would I be treated with respect, but I would also have the means to financially support my family as my father grew older. None of my siblings was pursuing a higher education, so if anyone was going to take care of the family, it would have to be me.

Another reason for pursuing a medical career in 1960s Vietnam was the Second Indochina War, known in the United States as the Vietnam War. I was quickly approaching draft age and would likely have been made a soldier if I hadn't been accepted into medical school (or some other higher institution of learning). As in the United States, college students in Vietnam received deferments.

At the time, there was only one medical school in Saigon: the Saigon University Medical School. Every year, the school accepted 150 to 200 new students, and admission decisions were based on the results of a single test. I spent months studying, devoting most of my free evenings and weekends to a study group with four other friends who were preparing for the exam as well. We all understood that if we failed, there was simply no way we would become doctors.

I was relieved when my test scores were high enough to get me into medical school. While basing admission on a single test might seem exceptionally restrictive when compared to admissions standards in other countries, there were also some major advantages that American medical students didn't share. Chief among those advantages was the fact that my education was completely financed by the South Vietnamese government. As long as I kept my grades at a passing level, I wouldn't have to worry about tuition expenses.

If I didn't keep my grades up, I would not only be dropped from the program but also immediately drafted into the military.

My first year of study was essentially what would be called pre-med in the United States—focused on basic sciences like biology, rather than anything specific about the human body. At that time, we were working with the French system of medicine; what this meant on a practical level is that we used French terminology when describing medical conditions and procedures.

After my first year, Saigon University switched over to the American system of medicine. Again, the chief difference in the American system was that medical conditions and treatments were described using English terminology. While this might seem to be a minor distinction, I still mix up French, English, and Vietnamese terms to this day, which can cause some confusion when speaking with other doctors (to say nothing of speaking with my patients). I'm sure that a deciding factor in making the switch from the French to the American system was the fact that American forces were occupying South Vietnam. While we had no American instructors in the program, we did have several instructors who had spent significant amounts of time in the United States studying medicine.

Beginning with the second year, we also began studying human anatomy. By this point, I truly enjoyed studying medicine. What had initially started as a way to bring honor back to my family (and avoid the draft) had become a genuine passion. In the third year, we switched from merely studying in classrooms to spending time in hospitals. I not only got to see how doctors worked firsthand, but also saw how their patients—and their peers—treated them with respect. This was a noble profession, and even if my family or the war hadn't been factors, I would have been proud to pursue it.

After six years of study, I graduated from medical school in 1974. Now that I was a doctor, I believed that my future was secure. I could restore a sense of honor to my family and take care of my father and siblings financially as they grew older. No matter what changes Vietnam was going through, there would always be a need for doctors, so my profession brought with it a sense of safety. Best of all, I would spend the rest of my life doing something that I'd grown to love.

Chapter Three

Before I began studying medicine, I was enrolled in the National Conservatory for Vietnamese Traditional Music. One of my high school teachers had noticed my talent for music and had recommended that I take an admission test. Like medical school, I was not required to pay anything to attend the National Conservatory, provided that I maintained passing grades. I began attending in 1965 and continued taking classes even when I began studying medicine at Saigon University. This wasn't as difficult as it might sound, since the music courses were taught in the evenings, while high school courses (and later, medical courses) were taught during the day. Given the tension at home following my parents' divorce, I didn't mind spending most of my time in one school or another. During those years, I usually only went home to sleep.

The teaching methods were informal, to say the least. Most of our courses consisted of listening to our instructors play pieces of music and then attempting to imitate what we heard. The "classrooms" were small rooms that had obviously been meant for storage or other functions; there was certainly no concern about acoustics. Each instructor used different recordings and different styles of teaching. Favoritism for certain students was an ongoing problem. We weren't even given sheet music to study. Basically, your quality of education depended entirely on which teacher you were assigned and how much that teacher favored you. These were the standards for teaching traditional Vietnamese music; they differed from those of Western music instruction, which was done with sheet music and a more formalized structure.

Many students found these standards unacceptable; in 1970, we organized a protest, demanding better and more uniform methods be employed by the instructors. As part of this protest, I wrote a letter to the minister of culture, explaining our grievances. To my surprise, the minister not only responded to my letter, but agreed with my opinions about how music should be taught.

I personally met with the minister of culture, and we discussed the specific problems facing the music program. The director of the program was present as well, and, while he objected to our protest, he also had to concede that the complaints were legitimate. At the end of the meeting, the minister agreed to implement a number of changes to the program, including larger classrooms that were more suitable for our studies and sheet music, which would bring a more uniform standard to the teaching methods. This was the first time I saw a positive change come about from my speaking up—a theme that would become important throughout my life, culminating in the United Airlines incident nearly fifty years later.

Unfortunately, as part of the agreement, I was told that I would have to leave the National Conservatory. Despite the minister agreeing that I was right to bring these problems to his attention, organizing the protest had marked me as a troublemaker (not the last time I would be given that label). And so I left the National Conservatory in 1970, never benefiting from the changes I'd helped to implement.

My love for music didn't end when I left school. I spent most of my days studying medicine, and while I no longer spent my nights at the National Conservatory, I devoted some time to music. I began composing songs of my own—expressions of the sadness I felt over losing my place at the National Conservatory. I wasn't performing anywhere, but I did submit three of these pieces to the National Prize contest for consideration. Looking back, I can't say how much hope I had of winning, but in fact one of them did win. The title of the winning song was "*Ta ve Ta tam Ao Ta*" ("You Come Back to Swim in Your Own Pond"). The song was my attempt to deal with my dismissal from the National Conservatory and focused on how we must take comfort in the things we have, rather than regretting the things we've lost or can never possess. The song was also a celebration of believing in oneself, a theme I would return to in other, nonmusical ways throughout my life.

Along with the prestige of winning the National Prize, I was also awarded money, which I immediately invested in starting a band with four of my friends. The band was called *Bach Viet*, and our style of music was largely influenced by the Beatles (a band that, while it had at the time recently broken up, was just being discovered by people in Vietnam), as well as traditional Vietnamese themes. At first, we played at college campuses and night clubs in Saigon. We were initially just happy to play and be heard by an audience, no matter how small. But we quickly gained in popularity, achieving a sort of local celebrity status. At one point, we released an album. We even began to perform once a year on television for an annual New Year's Day special.

While Bach Viet never became "the Vietnamese Beatles" by any stretch of the imagination, we did unfortunately fall into some of the same traps that led to the end of that band. Our problems boiled down to the root issue that most bands eventually encounter—ego. Our band had five members, and some thought they weren't as valued as others. Some members thought they were doing more of the work than others. All of us had different ideas concerning what direction the band should go. Each of us thought we deserved more credit for our individual contributions, leading to resentment and jealousy. Between the album and the television specials, the band began making some money…and money complicates relationships. I started Bach Viet in 1971, but three years later it was over.

By 1974, I was finishing up my medical studies, so it's difficult to say how much time I could have devoted to the band once I became a doctor. Still, my time spent with the National Conservatory and with Bach Viet helped me to maintain a balance in my life. I'm sure many people would be surprised to find out that I was able to attend two different schools simultaneously or that I was able to maintain high grades in medical school while also playing in a band. But for me, focusing exclusively on either music or medicine would have burned me out emotionally, while alternating between the two helped me take a break from each every day. Medical study was largely concerned with memorizing huge amounts of data, while at the same time learning to focus on the needs of patients. Music, on the other hand, was more free-form and allowed me to focus more on my own emotions and ideas. In the end, I believe that my medical studies helped me to compose and play better music, while my music helped me to better focus on my medical studies.

Once I became a doctor, performing music at a professional level was out of the question, although I continued to use music to help myself relax and to take my mind off other pressures in my life. And I'm happy to say that, even decades later, I still hear about people discovering Bach Viet and enjoying our music to this day.

Chapter Four

Since one of the reasons I wanted to study medicine was to avoid the draft, it's more than a little ironic that, immediately after graduating from medical school, I was drafted into the South Vietnam Army, specifically because my medical training gave me a valuable skill set that was needed by the military. Because I held a higher education degree upon entering the military, I was immediately given an officer's ranking: Lieutenant Medical Doctor. This rank brought me much respect and earned me a pay grade higher than that of soldiers recruited straight out of high school.

Furthermore, my military service ended up being far less dangerous than what most draftees found themselves doing. Medical personnel weren't in the line of fire nearly as often as other members of the military. My specific job involved training others in an army medical school, which placed me even farther away from the combat zones. It was a bit of an adjustment to go from being a student to becoming a teacher almost immediately upon graduation. After six years, I had a strong background in medical knowledge but had nowhere near the level of confidence that an experienced doctor might possess. Still, I adjusted to this new situation quickly.

Military service kept me away from my father and siblings, but this was no different than my time spent in medical school. My becoming a doctor had earned me respect, just as my winning the National

Prize for my music and the success of my band had brought respect. Serving in the military as an officer brought me even further respect. And yet, it seemed that the more respect I brought to my father and siblings, the less time I was able to spend with them.

This isn't to say that I was completely cut off from my family. One of my cousins, Hieu Trung Dang, lived near the military base where I taught, and I began to visit him almost daily. Like me, he'd been drafted into the military and was a major in the South Vietnam Navy. On many days, rather than making the long commute back to my father's house, I would simply stay with my cousin, having dinner with him and spending time with his wife and children.

Being drafted into the South Vietnam Army in the summer of 1974 would soon become significant. Rumors were circulating that the United States was planning to withdraw, and it was understood that, once South Vietnam lost the support of the United States, the war would certainly shift to North Vietnam's favor. In January of 1975, the rumors were confirmed, and many of us began making plans to leave Vietnam. Ordinarily, I wouldn't have had much cause to worry about which side won, since my medical background would be valued either way. But the fact that I'd actively served in the South Vietnam Army as an officer would have made me a target for retaliation, both from the new government and from incoming North Vietnamese citizens who'd served in the military in the north. On top of that, much of my education had focused on an American system of medicine, and the North Vietnamese would likely consider me to be "tainted" by American culture.

So I began making plans to leave Vietnam. As a major in the navy, my cousin had access to a small ship. Over the first four months of 1975, we discussed the possibility of his simply placing his family on board and sailing out of the country. Once the United States left, we imagined that there would be enough chaos in the area that we'd be able to flee the country without anyone trying to stop us. So I continued going to the army medical school every day, pretending that everything was going to be fine. I suppose thousands of us in Saigon (and across Vietnam) were doing the same thing: going about our daily tasks pretending everything would turn out for the best, all the while making plans to escape the moment the tide of battle turned.

Despite preparing for the day, I was still surprised when the end came so suddenly. On April 30, 1975, Saigon fell to the North Vietnamese Army and the Viet Cong. By the time I realized what was happening, roads leading out of the city were overflowing and it was impossible for me to reach my father, brothers, and sisters. Since I couldn't reach our house, I also couldn't pack anything, so I had to leave with what I was wearing and nothing more. I was barely able to make my way to my cousin's home. From there, I left with him and his family to the ship he had waiting for us. In addition to my cousin and his family, several other people nearby managed to make their way onto the ship before it left Saigon.

In total, I would say somewhere between fifty and eighty people crammed onto that ship, which had not been designed to carry that many people for any length of time. The chaos hadn't provided nearly as much cover as we'd hoped, and soldiers shot at the ship as we left port, forcing all of us to lie flat on the deck to provide the smallest targets possible to the land-bound soldiers. I honestly don't know if they were even North Vietnamese soldiers shooting at a South Vietnamese Navy ship or South Vietnamese soldiers shooting at deserters…not that it mattered much to us at the time. Change had come so suddenly that none of us had brought anything on board with us, and, even if we had, there wouldn't have been any room for food or water, much less clothing or valuables. And that's how I left Vietnam, sailing down the Saigon River on a stolen ship populated mostly by strangers, trying my best to avoid getting shot.

I remember watching Saigon burn and thinking that I would never be able to go back. The city could be and likely would be rebuilt, but I would not be welcomed back. I was worried about what would happen to my family. I had become a doctor to bring honor to my family, but now I wondered if my military service would make them targets of reprisal by the incoming government. This was 1975, and there was no Internet, no cell phones, nor any method for me to stay in contact with my family or even confirm whether they were all still alive. In the end, I could only look after myself and hope that they were able to do the same.

Our first stop after leaving Saigon was Côn Sơn Island, which had gained some infamy for the prison located there. Americans would likely only remember the area from the 1970 photo spread in *Life* showing the "tiger cages" where prisoners were kept. Since that photo spread had been published, the island had been occupied by US military forces. Over the previous year, it had been used as one of several transmitter sites for a radio station that provided weather and navigation data to ships and aircraft. In the days leading up to the fall of Saigon, the station continued providing such data to ships fleeing the area. By the time we reached the island, the equipment had burned out and the radio operators had fled. Strangely, what I remember most about the island was how peaceful it all seemed; the water surrounding it was clear and filled with turtles.

Unfortunately, we couldn't stay on the island for long. Any supplies that might have been left there by the radio operators had already been seized by the crews of other ships. We left the island in much the same condition as we'd arrived. After we left, we floated on that ship for several days. With no clocks or watches on board, I quickly lost track of time; I remember being hungry, thirsty, and worst of all, bored. We all had nothing to do and nothing to think about besides what we'd left behind.

Eventually, a US Navy ship picked us up. I wasn't surprised when many of my fellow passengers asked to be returned to Vietnam. Perhaps they'd had time to consider what sort of life would be waiting for them elsewhere, compared to the life they could have if they returned to the only home they'd ever known. Personally, I never considered going back. Besides my military service making me a target for reprisal back home, my medical background gave me some confidence that I would be able to find opportunities wherever I chose to go. I figured I had far more opportunities waiting for me in the United States than back in Vietnam. Those of us who chose to go on wished the returning ones luck, then we parted ways.

We were still packed in rather tightly on the US Navy ship, but there was enough food and water to go around, and we now had a clear destination. I knew that starting over in the United States wouldn't be easy, but I didn't expect the many false starts I'd make before finally finding my place in my new country.

Chapter Five

I've mentioned that much of my medical training involved an American system of medicine. This meant that I was already familiar with American medical terminology, which I believed would help me when I began practicing medicine in the United States. It also meant that I already had some exposure to the English language in general. While I was by no means fluent in English when I fled Saigon, I was able to communicate in basic terms with the naval personnel on the ship that picked us up. I was also able to translate what the personnel told me for other refugees who were not as fluent in English.

After several days at sea, we docked at Subic Bay in the Philippines. This is when the interview process began. Each of us was asked for our names, our former professions, and all manner of questions concerning why we'd left Vietnam. The United States was in the process of taking in hundreds of thousands of refugees from Vietnam, and while the admission process had to be streamlined to deal with the sheer number of people, it still felt as if the questions went on forever. After a couple days of stretching our legs on land and answering questions, we returned to the ship.

Our next stop was the US territory of Guam. Again, we spent a few days on shore answering questions and filling out paperwork. The fact that I not only had medical training but a medical degree from a school that specifically taught American medical terminology was of special interest to the people interviewing me. After a week, I was told that I was going to be relocated to a refugee camp in Indiantown Gap, Pennsylvania.

The camp was a series of converted military barracks. If you've seen any film about basic military training, then you have a good idea of what they looked like. Each barracks building had fifty bunk beds. The base where we were located must have had a hundred such barracks buildings, sheltering perhaps as many as ten thousand refugees. A separate building functioned as the dining hall, and yet another as the medical facility. I'd felt crowded on the ship that had brought me to the United States, but now I felt as if I was in a small town rather than a large camp.

I mention the medical facility because, with ten thousand people, there were several health issues at the refugee camp. I don't mean to suggest that we were treated badly, but when you get any large group of people together, accidents, sickness, and other health problems are bound to arise. The Red Cross had set up the medical clinic to treat the refugees, but, while the medical personnel at that clinic did a splendid job, few of them could speak Vietnamese, and none were fluent. Besides the language barrier, there was also a trust barrier. We had fled a hostile government in a country that we had known all our lives; now we were in a strange new country, dealing with a foreign government. Many of the refugees simply would not trust strangers they couldn't understand, so getting them to discuss personal health problems was difficult.

That is when my unique background and skill set became valuable to the Red Cross. I acted as an interpreter between refugees and medical personnel. I spoke to the medical personnel using American medical terminology, and I assured the refugees that the diagnoses they were being given were accurate. I was also able to ask the refugees follow-up questions that only someone with a medical background and a knowledge of the Vietnamese language would be able to ask. I was not licensed to practice medicine in the United

States at this point, but in many ways, this was my first real experience with practicing medicine (not just teaching it) after my graduation.

In later years, I would see a variety of ways in which American medicine and Vietnamese medicine were practiced differently, but even at the refugee shelter (which was not provided with cutting-edge medical facilities), I was surprised by some of the key differences. One of the first major differences I witnessed occurred when one of the refugees became pregnant. Working as an interpreter, I gathered more information and was better able to ease the woman's concerns than the American medical staff. Without going into too much detail, the woman told me that she did not wish to carry the fetus to term: she wanted an abortion. Today, this would probably seem like a fairly straightforward procedure, but in 1975, the *Roe v. Wade* decision was only two years old. In Vietnam, abortions were still mostly illegal, and the only time a doctor could perform one was during a spontaneous abortion, that is, when the woman's body was already rejecting the fetus, essentially assisting her in order to minimize the risk to her health. These legal limitations had driven many women to extreme actions in order to force their bodies to "spontaneously" reject the fetus. But in the United States, we were able to send this woman to a medical center to have the abortion performed safely without such extreme measures.

While the Red Cross and other volunteers did what they could for us, nobody was happy to be in a refugee camp. Each of us had to remain there until somebody would sponsor us. Since most of us didn't know anyone in the United States and we weren't able to travel freely through the country, we couldn't look for sponsors. This was in the time before the Internet, so there was no way for us to search for potential sponsors while remaining at the camp. We simply had to wait for sponsors to find us. For the most part, the sponsors were representatives from Lutheran, Baptist, and Catholic charity organizations.

Despite our situation, most of us preferred being in the United States to Vietnam. Since the fall of Saigon, stories had found their way to us of the terrible conditions that many of the people now had to live under there. Even if half of what we were hearing were unfounded rumors, few of us wanted to go back. I still remember the night we sang "God Bless America" on July 4, 1975, our first American Independence Day celebration.

After three months in the refugee camp, my cousin, his family, and I were sponsored by a Baptist church in Columbia, South Carolina. The church placed us in a three-bedroom apartment, which was more comfortable than the refugee camp. There were still seven of us, so it didn't provide that much more in the way of privacy, but we were glad to finally be taking another step toward a more permanent life in the United States. We all continued to improve our English language skills; while reading and writing came quickly, speaking English required more practice. My cousin was also learning to drive a car, and all of us attended church services on Sundays. Beyond attending church functions, we mostly stayed in the apartment.

I had also begun attending church chorus practices every Wednesday, so I could sing during the Sunday services. Surprisingly, it was my music background (and not my far more extensive medical background) that led me to my first proper career in the United States. Dr. Lee Bruckner, the pastor of the church that had sponsored us, invited me to teach ethnomusicology at the University of Washington.

Such an invitation should have been a dream come true, especially given all the hardships I'd gone through in previous months. But at around the same time, I also received a letter about my medical license application, presenting me with a dilemma. I was required to take several courses and tests before I could legally practice medicine in the United States. But there was no way I'd be able to support myself without help while I focused on the training and testing for the medical license, and it was clear that the Baptist church sponsoring me had no intention of continuing to support me during that process. Though I would have preferred to pursue my medical career first, the teaching position was open immediately.

So I left for Seattle in September of 1975, my third relocation in five months.

Chapter Six

After three months in a refugee camp and another month sharing an apartment with six people, you might imagine that I'd welcome the chance to get a place of my own. But leaving South Carolina was heartbreaking.

In April, I'd left Vietnam, the only country I'd ever lived in. I'd left my father, mother, brothers, and sisters in a country that was undergoing so much upheaval that I had no way of knowing if they were even still alive. Most of the people at the refugee camp were strangers to me, but we all had the shared experience of having lived in Vietnam. When I moved to South Carolina, I was still sharing an apartment with family members, so I never felt alone. But now, I was relocating to a city I'd never seen, staying with people I'd never met, and surrounded by people who had never been to Vietnam and didn't speak Vietnamese. Moving to Seattle was the first time in my life that I felt truly alone.

But as in Indiantown Gap and Columbia, there were people in Seattle who were willing to help me adjust to another major change in my life. When I arrived there, I was welcomed by Dr. Lieberman, a music director at the University of Washington. I stayed with his family during my first week in the city while we searched for a suitable apartment for me.

I think it's important to acknowledge all the people who helped me in those early months, from the US Navy, the Red Cross, and the Baptist church to Seattle and the University of Washington. I encountered hundreds of men and women who offered their time, their money, and even their homes to strangers simply because they believed it was the right thing to do. Despite everything I'd gone through since leaving Vietnam and despite feeling increasingly alone with each successive move, I was always aware of what all these people did for me and will always remember them. I experienced firsthand how welcoming America could be to refugees and immigrants.

That said, I cried every day during my first week in Seattle. I never regretted leaving Vietnam, and I knew I would experience difficulties in moving to a new country. But I hadn't realized how isolated I would feel, despite all the people helping me every step of the way. While I had a decent grasp of the English language, I wasn't completely fluent, and I could tell that most Americans had difficulty understanding me. Between the language barrier and the lack of people with a common experience, I simply had nobody that I could talk to about what I was feeling. On top of that, I'd expected to make my living in America as a doctor and now I was going to teach music.

After a week living with the music director, I moved into my own apartment. It was the first time that I'd had my own place since leaving Vietnam. The feeling of isolation depressed me, but I had a new job to occupy my thoughts and not much time to prepare before the beginning of classes. Fortunately, the apartment was near enough to the university that I didn't need to drive, which was convenient since I didn't own a car. In fact, beyond a few sets of clothes, I arrived in Seattle with no possessions. After four months, I'd learned how to live without possessions, so my apartment was mostly empty when I began teaching.

The ethnomusicology class focused on traditional Vietnamese music. In many ways, it was similar to the courses I'd taken back in Vietnam. Five years previously, I'd been expelled from the National

Conservatory. Now I was a teacher, with the opportunity to provide a better course in traditional Vietnamese music in America than what had been offered to me in Vietnam.

Looking back, I can see why someone might have placed me in a position as a music teacher rather than a doctor. I had no experience practicing medicine. After graduating from medical school, I was immediately drafted as a teacher for other medical students. My only other significant accomplishment outside of earning a medical degree was forming an award-winning band. Anyone looking at my background would have seen an accomplished musician and an experienced teacher with no professional medical experience.

Still, teaching music in the United States was quite different from teaching medicine in Vietnam. I wanted to reach out to the other traditional Vietnamese music instructors at the university, compare methods, and get a feel for what would be expected of me. Unfortunately, upon arriving on campus, I found that no other instructors taught my particular subject.

During my first semester, I taught a class with only fifteen students. The university supplied us with traditional Vietnamese musical instruments and sheet music. I couldn't help but compare this course to the one I'd taken as a student, where sheet music wasn't even provided.

After three months of study, my class joined with the classes studying traditional Chinese music and traditional Indian music for a recital performed in front of both students and faculty. I even participated by performing a piece on a monochord (a Vietnamese one-string instrument). The recital received a standing ovation.

My second semester of teaching saw the class size double to thirty. With each lesson, I grew more confident in my teaching ability and more comfortable with my new life. There's an old adage that teachers can learn as much from their students as their students can learn from them, and in my case, that was especially true, as I sharpened my English language skills day by day. As my understanding of the language increased, I felt more at ease talking with other people and my sense of loneliness faded.

I also reformed my band, Bach Viet, at the end of 1975. The new members were two students from my first class, Sandy Bradley (already a well-known musician) and Allan Swenson (a graduate student who had recently returned from a stint with the Peace Corps). Our song list was a combination of traditional Vietnamese and American folk music. Back in Vietnam, the Beatles had been a huge influence on my work. But in mid-1970s America, folk music was popular, especially among college campuses, so that was what influenced this new version of my band. We performed for the next year at college campuses in Washington, Oregon, and California.

While I was teaching music, playing music, and settling into my new American life, I hadn't forgotten about my medical career. After many exchanges with the American Medical Association, I was finally offered a chance to take the Education Commission for Foreign Medical Graduates (ECFMG) exam. Passing it would allow me to work as a general practitioner in the United States, but I would need to spend several months preparing to take the test. Fortunately, my contract with the University of Washington had just expired and the AMA had already made living arrangements for me in Loma Linda, California (where the test would be conducted). So, I moved once again.

Chapter Seven

I'd never truly settled into my apartment in Seattle. I'd arrived without any possessions besides some clothes. Even the instruments I played had been provided by the university. And while an instructor's pay was adequate, I hadn't furnished my apartment in a lavish way. I'd learned to live simply, so when it came time to move once again, I found both packing and settling into another new place relatively easy.

Once again, an organization provided for my room and board, this time Loma Linda University. I shared the apartment with three other refugees who also wanted to practice medicine in the United States. Since we were all focused on our studies and had similar backgrounds, there was no conflict between us, and living together was easy enough.

Every day, we took a bus to the university to study for the ECFMG test. A great deal of this studying involved an instructor going over American medical terminology. Since I had already been taught these terms, this ended up feeling more like a refresher course than a traditional lesson. Still, I didn't take anything for granted.

The test itself was nothing remarkable—written and verbal portions given over a day, not unlike most other college examinations. It would be several months before I was told whether I had passed. If I failed the test, I could attempt to take it again, but in the meantime,

I had no job, no license to practice medicine in the United States, and no teaching position. On top of that, now that I had finished studying for the test, I was to vacate the university's apartment.

For the first time since my arrival in the United States over a year earlier, I had nowhere to go and no organization to turn to. I moved back to Seattle to wait for the results of my ECFMG test and rented an apartment with a couple of friends who were also refugees looking for work. I also looked up Sandy and Allen, and we reformed Bach Viet for the third time (counting the original version in Vietnam).

For the next year, I lived off what I could earn as a musician. It wasn't much money, but the band had built enough of a reputation that we were able to keep a regular schedule of performances around Washington.

Even when the AMA finally contacted me to let me know that I'd passed the ECFMG, I continued to pursue my music career, since passing that test was only the first obstacle I had to face in establishing a practice in the United States. Besides my work with the Red Cross, I had no experience practicing medicine. Despite my improved language skills, I still had an accent that many non-Vietnamese would find difficult to understand. I had no money to rent an office, much less to purchase basic medical equipment or hire a support staff. If I started a general practice, I would have no easy means to draw in people as patients. I needed to get a job with a hospital before I could hope to open my own practice, and that meant I needed to take more tests and go through more training.

I'd applied for the Federal Licensing Examination (FLEX), but the next exam would not be administered for several months. Passing this exam would make getting work at an American hospital much easier. Unlike the ECFMG, I was able to study for this exam on my own without needing to relocate.

During this time, I was also maintaining contact with other Vietnamese refugees in the area. After the Vietnam War, hundreds of thousands of refugees had moved to the United States. I knew

that my own difficulties paled in comparison to what other refugees
went through. I'd come alone, in excellent physical health, and with
a strong educational and medical background. Others had come with
young children and elderly relatives to care for. Many of them had
health problems (either from a preexisting condition or because of
the hardships of traveling to the United States). Many had little or
no education. If I was having a hard time adjusting and making ends
meet, what about them?

I'd been helped by so many people and organizations since
arriving in the United States, I decided that it was time I helped
someone else too. If I had a medical practice, I could have offered to
help treat refugees. But at the time, I was a musician…so that would
be how I'd help.

I began organizing the International Music Festival in the summer
of 1978. I did so with the goal of raising money to help refugees, while
also generating interest in and respect for Vietnamese music and
culture. I scheduled the event to take place during National Art Night
and invited local Vietnamese musicians to perform. I was interviewed
by several local magazines about the event and even got support from
the mayor of Seattle. The venue for the festival could seat a maximum
of three thousand people, and we anticipated a sold-out show.

Then the backlash began.

Since many of the musicians I'd invited were from Vietnam,
several of them noticed that the date of the festival was September 2,
which coincided with the Vietnamese Independence Day celebrated
by Vietnam's communist government. People questioned why I
had scheduled the event on that particular day and suggested that
I was showing support for the communist takeover of my home
country. The date was simply the only one available at the venue
I wanted, and I honestly had not made the connection until it was
pointed out to me. By the time I realized what the date symbolized for
many refugees, it was too late to reschedule. Since I'd fled Vietnam
for the same reasons as many other refugees and believed that my

involvement with Saigon University would have made me a special target of the incoming communist government, the suggestion that I was celebrating that government was especially hurtful.

By the day of the festival, 50 percent of the purchased tickets had been returned for refunds. Still, I considered the three-hour concert to be a success; after subtracting all the expenses, I found that we'd broken even. We had no money to give to the refugees, but I hoped that the concert at least gave people a stronger appreciation for Vietnamese culture.

I left the concert that night and immediately went to an emergency room. The difficulties of setting up the concert and dealing with the backlash and accusations had put me under a lot of stress. I'd also been studying for my medical exam, looking for gigs for Bach Viet, and trying to secure a job in the medical field—all at the same time. I was unsurprised to discover that I'd developed a bleeding ulcer. Unfortunately, since I had no money or health insurance, I couldn't stay at the hospital and decided to simply go back to my apartment and spend a couple of days recuperating.

When I got home, I discovered that my apartment had been broken into and my few possessions (clothes and musical instruments) had been stolen. So I spent the next couple of days sleeping in an empty apartment, passing black stool, and ignoring phone calls.

Three months later, I passed the FLEX. Around that same time, one of my roommates shared that his uncle, a physician in Indiana, had heard about a position that he thought would be perfect for me. Uncle Joe set it all up, and I began 1979 by packing my few possessions and taking a train across the country to my new job. Things hadn't gone exactly as I'd planned, but I was finally going to live my dream of being a physician. I was going to find my dream in Michigan City, Indiana.

I would be working in the Indiana State Prison.

Chapter Eight

Once again, I found myself in a new city with no friends, no money, and a more or less empty apartment. Despite having lived in America for three and a half years, I felt like I was starting from scratch once again. But that wasn't entirely true—I was finally able to practice medicine in the United States. I also had enough of a social network that I'd secured a job without an interview.

At first, work at the Indiana State Prison was fairly mundane. I performed basic routine examinations of the inmates, treated minor injuries, and prescribed medication. In some ways, it was like being a general practitioner, except that I didn't have to actively seek out patients or worry about them switching to another physician.

Most young doctors don't dream of working in a prison. The pay was certainly better than what I earned as a teacher or a musician, but it was still on the low side compared to what a physician could make in other circumstances. The environment was depressing—none of my patients were ever happy with their situation, since after all, they were prisoners—and because I was the only doctor on staff, I didn't have any professional peers there with me on the job. Still, the prison staff treated me well, and it was satisfying to finally work as a professional physician.

Soon, the mundane nature of the job lulled me into a false sense of security. At some point, I stopped thinking of the inmates as criminals and simply treated them as if they were any other patients. So when one of them asked for pain medication one day and I refused, I thought that would be the end of that conversation. He'd come into the clinic complaining about chest pains and demanding that I give him a morphine shot. After a quick exam, I determined that the pain didn't require such an extreme narcotic and instead recommended that he take some ibuprofen. I was surprised when he grabbed hold of my stethoscope, then shocked when he wrapped it around my neck and began to choke me. To this day, I don't know if he was simply angry with me or if he thought that strangling me would somehow make me change my mind.

While I survived the attack with minimal injury, I knew that I couldn't continue working at the prison. Fortunately, the warden was not only understanding but knew about another position elsewhere in the state that he felt would be a better fit for me—at the Muscatatuck Hospital in North Vernon, Indiana. I was already familiar with that hospital because that was where Uncle Joe worked.

And so, after only two months of living in Michigan City, I packed my belongings and moved once again. This would be my seventh relocation in four years. I hadn't lived in Michigan City long enough to make any friends, so the move occurred without ceremony.

The Muscatatuck Hospital mostly dealt with patients with mental disabilities. In many ways, the work was similar to what I had done at the Indiana State Prison. I would conduct routine physical examinations, prescribe medication, and treat various injuries. I worked at an outpatient clinic, but a separate wing functioned like a traditional hospital for the more serious cases. And like the prison, many of the patients lived permanently at the hospital.

Despite what had happened to me at the prison, I was never afraid of any of the patients who came to see me at the hospital. I know that many people feel uneasy around those with mental disabilities (in much the same way that many people feel uncomfortable around prisoners), but I was never threatened by anyone during the year I worked there. And unlike the prison, I was never alone with any of my patients; a social worker was always present.

The social worker wasn't there to protect me from my patients, however. In fact, the truth was quite the opposite. While I came to trust and respect most of my coworkers at the hospital, unfortunately, cases of patient abuse arose from time to time. I remember one particular case when I was treating a woman who turned out to be pregnant. Despite my own efforts and those of the social worker, we were never able to get her to identify the man who had impregnated her. In fact, I don't know if she was even aware of who had done it. But whoever was responsible had obviously understood that he would never be identified due to the woman's severe disability. We knew that it was probably a staff member because the woman was a resident of our hospital, and access to the hospital was limited. While she was transferred to another hospital immediately after the pregnancy was discovered, the identity of the staff member at fault was never discovered. This was the late 1970s, when neither sexual assault nor the mistreatment of those with mental disabilities were taken as seriously as they are today, and, at that time, it was not possible to absolutely confirm paternity with a DNA test.

Another key difference between work at the hospital and the prison was that I wasn't the only doctor on staff. Five other physicians worked at Muscatatuck. All of them were Vietnamese, so we came from similar backgrounds and had similar training. We were able to discuss both medical issues and more personal issues concerning life in the United States as immigrants.

While I found my work at the Muscatatuck Hospital fulfilling, I knew I wouldn't be staying there indefinitely. During the year I worked there, I applied for residency programs at several universities. Eventually, I was accepted for residency training at the University of Louisville.

The administrative staff at the hospital were understanding about my desire to move on to new opportunities. By my last day on the job, they had already hired my replacement, another Vietnamese refugee starting a new life in the United States. In fact, the last thing I did for the hospital was drive to the airport to pick up my replacement.

As it turned out, that trip to the airport would change my life more than anything else that had happened since my move to the United States.

Chapter Nine

Dung Truong was also a doctor who'd fled Vietnam after the communist takeover. We had both studied medicine at Saigon University, and she was one year ahead of me. No doubt we had seen one another there more than once, but we had both been so intent on our studies that we had never noticed each other.

Perhaps the biggest difference in our experiences was that Dung Truong hadn't left Vietnam until 1978, whereas I'd managed to get out of the country on the day Saigon fell. Whereas I'd only heard rumors about what was happening in the country since the communist takeover, she had lived through three years of it before finally managing to escape. She told me about it while I drove her from the airport to North Vernon.

She'd spent her three years in communist-controlled South Vietnam, working in a hospital. The work itself wasn't much different from what she'd done before the takeover, but she was also required to attend a daily lecture about communism. Many of these lectures included condemnations of South Vietnam; she was never allowed to forget that she lived in the part of the country that had lost the war. During those years, she secretly collected what little money she could tuck away, saving up until she could pay someone to get her out of the country. Thousands of other people were also attempting to flee.

Eventually, she accumulated enough money to buy her way onto a ship. The journey itself was more dangerous than what I'd gone through four years earlier. At the time when I escaped, things were in enough disarray that ships could get out of the country with little danger of being stopped by the Vietnamese government (which was still securing power on the mainland). By the time Dung Truong left, though, the government was on the lookout for people trying to get out; if she'd been caught, she would have been sent to prison. In addition, the boats on which many refugees escaped were in poor repair and could easily be destroyed by harsh weather or powerful waves. There was also the threat of Malaysian pirates seizing the ship; if they boarded a vessel, they would more likely than not simply murder the passengers in order to take the ship itself.

Despite all these dangers, she managed to reach Indonesia, where she waited for six months until a sponsor could be found in the United States. By the time she arrived in San Jose, she had no intention of ever returning to Vietnam.

During my five years in the United States, I had worked with plenty of Vietnamese refugees, both as a music teacher and a doctor. And Dung Truong was certainly not the first woman doctor I'd met. I'd expected to meet a fellow doctor and refugee, someone I could have a pleasant conversation with and then never see again.

What I hadn't expected was to meet someone so beautiful. Obviously, plenty of doctors were beautiful women, but I'd never noticed any of them. But now, I was escorting an intelligent, driven, and beautiful woman to her new job.

I'd dated women since moving to this country, but I'd never been involved in a serious relationship (before or after leaving Vietnam). Between my studies, my career, and the fact that I had to relocate on average every six months, I hadn't had much opportunity to even consider a long-term relationship. And until I'd met Dung Truong, I'd never had much desire to do so.

To say that what happened between us was love at first sight wouldn't be completely true. It actually took an hour-long drive from the Indianapolis Airport to her new apartment before I realized that Dung Truong would one day be my wife. There was at least one immediate problem facing any relationship between us: as soon as I dropped her off, I had to go back to my own apartment to pack. I was not only leaving a job; I was leaving Indiana. Luckily, Louisville was only an hour's drive from North Vernon.

Moving to Kentucky was a simple enough process, and the residency program was rather straightforward. Once or twice a week, I got to see patients. While my hours changed week to week, I was never on call during the weekends. The program was three years long, and at the end of each year, I would be evaluated; a decision would be made concerning whether or not I got to stay on.

Since my weekends were always free, I left Louisville every Friday evening to see Dung Truong. And while both of us were making decent money at our respective jobs, there simply wasn't much to do in North Vernon. Sometimes we'd take a day trip to Indianapolis or Columbus, but for the most part we were content to spend our time together at her apartment.

While we were both doing well at our jobs, problems with living in America still came up. Some of these problems boiled down to simple prejudice; for example, at the end of my first year of residency at the University of Louisville, I was called into the director's office and told that I would not be kept on for a second year. While I knew that many residents were let go after their first year in the program, this decision still took me by surprise. As far as I knew, none of the patients or staff had ever had a problem with me, and I couldn't recall any major mistake I'd made during my first year. When I asked the director why I was being let go, he said that the language barrier impaired my work.

My English was fairly limited, but after working at the University of Washington, the Indiana State Prison, and the Muscatatuck

Hospital, this was the first time that anyone had suggested it was so bad that I couldn't do my job. My command of the language had increased during each of those jobs. I couldn't believe that after five years in the United States, my English was suddenly not good enough. And I'd heard no complaints during my year at the University of Louisville. So I asked to see my performance report.

The director turned over the report, and a quick review showed no complaints about my performance. Nor was there any mention of a "language barrier." From what I could tell, this was the director's opinion, backed by no evidence. Once I'd looked over the report, he conceded that there was no real problem with my work and that I could stay for another year.

The whole exchange was bizarre in how blatantly it was based on prejudice. Because I was from Vietnam, some people assumed I wouldn't be able to speak English and that there would be multiple complaints against me. The director hadn't even bothered to look through the report before making his decision. And getting him to change his mind was as simple as saying no and asking him to check the records. While some of the fights in my life had been long, drawn-out affairs, some were won by simply asking someone to check again. This was another important and life-changing lesson that was on my mind on that flight in 2017.

As it turned out, there was more than just a principle at stake. I needed to stay in the residency program. While I'd survived on the goodwill of charity organizations and my music career in the past, I knew that I needed a career that was more stable and lucrative in the future—and not only for myself. Six months after we'd begun dating, Dung Truong found out she was pregnant. So during the second year of my residency training, we would have a son to support.

Chapter Ten

Both of us were excited to become parents. We would need to juggle our respective schedules and make the usual sacrifices, but neither of us had any family in the United States, so this was our chance to build a new family together.

Before the baby was born, we were married. We chose to have a small, informal gathering of friends to announce our marriage and Dung Truong's pregnancy. The legal wedding ceremony took place in a Louisville court with no guests in attendance. We were both doing all right financially, but we agreed that a lavish wedding ceremony was beyond our means, especially since we were already saving for the various expenses that would come once the baby was born.

At this point, Dung Truong also legally changed her name to Teresa Dao, both as a way to symbolize a new stage in her life and an attempt to further blend in with American culture. Despite our background, we both considered ourselves to be Americans now.

Teresa applied for the pediatric residency program at the University of Louisville and was admitted. This meant we wouldn't need to make an hour-long commute to see each other any longer. By the time the baby was born, we were living together in an apartment in Louisville.

Timothy Dao was born on May 26, 1982. Like Teresa, his name was an Americanized version of a Vietnamese name. In Vietnamese, his name was Tam, which is also the word for "heart." We gave him that name for two reasons, the first being that he represented the love between his mother and myself.

The other reason for our son's name was a bit more elaborate. Back in Vietnam, Teresa had been a cardiologist—a heart specialist. Once she came to the United States, she'd chosen to specialize in pediatrics for the same reason I'd chosen internal medicine: because there were more opportunities. On top of that, a cardiology residency would take six years to complete.

But like me, Teresa never once regretted leaving her career in Vietnam behind. We both had to make sacrifices when we came to this country, but we gained far more than we'd hoped. We were both in residency programs, we had a healthy son, and our future together looked bright.

Immediately after our son was born, Teresa took time off from her residency to be with him. However, there was never a question about whether she was going to be a stay-at-home mother. Like me, Teresa had worked hard to earn her medical degree, and she had no intention of giving that up now that she was a mother. When she returned to work, we devised a system where the days we were on call were synchronized so that when one of us was dealing with patients, the other one would be home with the baby. For those times when we both had to work, we paid the landlady to watch our son.

And for anyone who wonders whether a name can influence a child's life, our son Timothy would grow up to become a cardiologist.

Chapter Eleven

After Timothy was born, our lives settled into a busy but manageable routine. Fortunately, we were both working, so money wasn't a problem for us. It's true that the baby brought many additional expenses, but the fact is that Teresa and I had both grown accustomed to surviving on little money, between our time in Vietnam during and after the war, as well as living as refugees in the United States, so it didn't feel like much of a sacrifice to us. Between our respective careers and our responsibilities to the baby, however, the days could become exhausting.

Six months after Timothy was born, once we were firmly entrenched in a routine, Teresa became pregnant once again. Not only did we both need to keep working, but we also needed to make allowances for a second child. That meant more bills, more time spent away from our jobs, and more favors called in for friends to watch our children.

In addition, I was starting my third and final year of residency training at the University of Louisville. I'd passed my second-year evaluation without a repeat of what had happened the year before. Once my residency was finished, I would need to find employment elsewhere. In fact, I would need to find employment before school was finished so I wouldn't have any lengthy downtime with no money coming in. I knew that Teresa would need to take some time off after the second baby was born, so I would also have to be the sole provider for a family of four, at least for a little while.

Given the performance reviews I was receiving, I had no doubt that I would be able to find something in my field. In fact, as long as there were no further surprises, I was confident that I would earn enough money to take care of myself, my wife, and both of our children.

Teresa gave birth to twins: Crystal and Christine Dao were born on August 23, 1983. Anyone who's had children will understand the mixture of surprise, joy, and dread that I felt when I was told that we'd been blessed with *two* beautiful babies, with no idea at the time how Teresa and I were going to manage to juggle this unexpected additional responsibility.

Chapter Twelve

After Crystal and Christine were born, Teresa took some more time off from her residency training to take care of them. But even with three small children, neither of us could put our careers on hold for too long. Not only had we sacrificed too much to give up on our dreams, but the financial demands of raising three children meant that we needed to have a double-income household.

Even with two incomes, raising three children wasn't easy. For one thing, we were still living in the two-bedroom apartment that we'd rented when we thought we would only be raising one child. Now Timothy, Crystal, and Christine were all sharing one bedroom. And as anyone who's raised more than one child knows, when one of them woke up crying in the middle of the night, they'd *all* wake up crying in the middle of the night. Soothing them back to sleep was often a two-person job, so there was none of the usual "it's your turn" excuse that we could make when there was only one child.

When I'd first left the refugee camp to stay in an apartment in South Carolina, I'd had to share it with seven other people. Those conditions had been cramped with occasional middle-of-the-night wake-ups, but I'd known then that it would only be temporary. Also, at the time, I hadn't so badly needed a full night's sleep in order to properly carry out a medical career.

Still, between our schedule juggling, day care, and the babysitting our landlady did for us, we made it work. We both knew the current situation couldn't last indefinitely. As the children grew older, they would need their own separate bedrooms. The residency programs wouldn't last forever, either, so we'd need to secure other types of jobs.

It might seem strange that, once my internal medicine residency was finished in 1984, I immediately began a fellowship, this time in pulmonary medicine. Ordinarily, once a residency is finished, most doctors either sign on with a hospital or a group practice, or they go off to start a practice of their own. However, joining another practice or hospital often requires the newly hired doctor to relocate, and, with my wife's residency program only half finished, we had to stay in Louisville. The pulmonary medicine program was based at the University of Louisville Hospital, which provided several advantages at the time. I was already familiar with the hospital and many of its staff members. Staying at the same hospital meant that we didn't have to relocate once again (which would have been really difficult with three children, even if Teresa's residency hadn't been a factor). Since it was a two-year program, I would end up finishing it around the same time that Teresa finished her pediatric residency program, at which point we'd both be free to move elsewhere.

Sticking with the same location also meant that I wouldn't have to prove myself again. The evaluation I'd gone through during my first year of internal medicine residency still weighed on my mind, and I knew that every time I had to start over, there would be someone ready to say I was unqualified because of my Vietnamese background. I knew that Teresa had to deal with the same prejudice from time to time. In fact, during her first-year pediatric residency evaluation, Teresa had been denied a second year in the program due to a "language barrier." However, remembering what I'd told her about my own experience with this excuse, she'd asked to see her evaluation records. And like me, there had been no complaints concerning her grasp of English. So, also like me, she was allowed to continue with the program simply because she'd asked for proof.

Teresa was in a different residency program than I'd been in, which meant that, despite being in the same hospital, she was dealing with a different director. So this was not a matter of one single bigoted director or misunderstanding. It was an assumption held by multiple authority figures at the hospital that simply being a Vietnamese refugee made us unfit to practice medicine in the United States. There is some irony in the fact that part of the reason we'd fled Vietnam was the prejudice we had suffered for being South Vietnamese and "corrupted" by American influence and culture, only to come here and find that we were viewed with suspicion by Americans for being too influenced by Vietnamese culture and language. And I can't even dismiss this as just a problem with the University of Louisville Hospital, since I also heard similar stories while working with Vietnamese musicians in Seattle and Vietnamese doctors at the Muscatatuck Hospital.

This sort of situation is nothing new. Whenever a significant number of refugees enter a new country, they are often viewed with suspicion and hostility. I'm sure that many native-born Americans believed that refugees were taking their jobs and expecting handouts. But the fact is that both Teresa and I (as well as thousands of other refugees) had to essentially start over once we arrived in this country, recertifying for careers we'd already trained for in Vietnam. We knew that refugees weren't "taking" anything they hadn't earned. In fact, many of us literally worked twice as many years to get the same things as those born in this country. I've seen this same prejudice and these same false arguments directed toward other groups of refugees (Somalians, Syrians, Haitians). And like us, I'm sure they all hope that their children won't have to work as hard or face as much prejudice as they have to earn their own place in this country.

But for the time being, I was in a relatively secure position. My pulmonary medicine fellowship went much the same way as my internal medicine residency training. My subspecialty was in critical care. I was on call a couple times a week and taking further medical training the rest of the time. Again, my schedule was flexible enough that I could coordinate with my wife so at least one of us was at home with our children.

Near the end of the first year of my pulmonary medicine fellowship, we found out that Teresa was pregnant once again. Our fourth child, Benjamin, was born on September 22, 1985. My wife took some time off after giving birth, and we once again found a way to coordinate our schedules to accommodate our children's needs. But it was growing more difficult to make ends meet for our growing family.

By 1986, I was approaching the end of my pulmonary medicine fellowship and Teresa was approaching the end of her pediatric residency; it had taken her longer than expected due to the time she'd had to take off for two pregnancies. At this point, our oldest child, Timothy, was already in preschool. Between our flexible schedules and day care, we'd established a system where our children always had someone watching them, while we were able to make enough money to support them. On top of that, now six of us were living in the same apartment where we'd originally moved in as a family of three. Not only did we need more money, but we also needed a bigger place to live. So, with my fellowship and Teresa's residency about to end, it was time for us to make yet another major change in our lives.

Chapter Thirteen

After five years of working through a residency program and a fellowship, I had made my fair share of friends at the University of Louisville Hospital; not only social friends, but also colleagues who were familiar with my medical work and could recommend me for other positions. One such friend offered me a unique opportunity in 1986.

Dr. Lon Keith, who was one of my cardiologist fellows at the hospital, had gotten to know me during my pulmonary medicine fellowship. He knew that once my fellowship was finished, I would need a job, and he presented me with an amazing opportunity. In addition to his work as a cardiologist, he also maintained a practice in Elizabethtown, Kentucky. One of his associates, Dr. Leichenberger, also had an internal medicine practice in Elizabethtown and was getting ready to retire. Rather than simply shutting down the practice, Dr. Leichenberger wanted to find someone who could take it over. Dr. Keith had suggested that he get in contact with me.

It takes years to build a successful medical practice. People tend to have a family physician whom they learn to trust over decades. Most of a doctor's early clients are people who have recently moved to the area because of a job or other major life change. Over time, those patients might recommend the doctor to other people, as well as bring their children and spouses. But while a healthy practice is

usually built one patient at a time, it can be lost far more quickly. A
single bad experience can not only drive a person to switch primary
care physicians, but to recommend that their family, friends, and
coworkers do the same. A successful medical practice is something
that is cultivated and maintained over decades, and it is a tremendous
sign of trust when one doctor chooses to hand it over to another.
A physician grows to care about the clients in his practice, so
handing over that practice is essentially trusting another doctor with
their lives.

All of which is to say that I was honored that I had earned that
level of trust and that I didn't enter into a decision to take over the
practice hastily. Among other things, taking over the practice would
require that I relocate my family to another city. Teresa and I had
been living in Louisville for several years at that point, and while both
of us had experience relocating to new cities (not to mention new
countries), things were different now. We had four children. We had
friends in Louisville whom we could trust to babysit our children. We
had found day care centers that we trusted as well. Our oldest child
was in preschool and making friends. And we were familiar with
the Vietnamese community in the area. Moving to Elizabethtown
would involve building an entirely new network of professional and
personal contacts.

But the fact was that Teresa and I both had to find new jobs soon,
and the opportunity being presented to me was simply too good to
pass up. Once both of our residencies were finished, we rented a
small house in Elizabethtown in July of 1986. It was a beautiful three-
bedroom rental property, which provided us with some much-needed
extra space. There was even a backyard, which might not seem like a
luxury to many, but meant a great deal to two refugees who'd spent
the last few years moving from one tiny apartment to another.

The neighborhood was firmly middle class, and I was glad to
see that our neighbors were friendly and welcoming. Many of them
were just like us, starting families of their own and renting their first

homes. We grew to trust them so much that I hired our next-door neighbor Julia to be the office manager at my practice.

When I first took over Dr. Leichenberger's practice, he was still seeing patients. For the first few weeks, he continued to meet with his regular patients but introduced me to them as well when they came in, telling them that he was leaving and that I would be taking over the practice. While I'm sure most of his patients would have preferred that he continued in his medical practice, I could also tell that most of them were at least willing to give me a chance. After a few weeks of breaking the news to patients one by one, he eventually left me on my own. At first, I was seeing around ten patients a day, and, for the most part, they were happy with me as a replacement and stayed with the practice. In fact, I gained a number of referrals in those early months, and the practice grew significantly.

At the same time, I was working full time at Hardin Memorial Hospital as a pulmonary specialist. While this didn't leave me with any free time, it did mean that Teresa and I didn't have to worry about money.

And while I was building up my medical practice, Teresa was interviewing for pediatrician positions in the area. Eventually, she secured a job at the Ireland Army Hospital in Fort Knox—yes, the same Fort Knox where the United States Bullion Depository (containing a significant portion of the country's gold reserve) is located. The hospital dealt primarily with active-duty personnel located in Kentucky, Indiana, Illinois, Michigan, Ohio, and Wisconsin. Included along with those active-duty servicemembers were their children, hence the need for a sizable pediatric department.

One of the advantages of being a pediatrician is probably that supervisors tend to be more sympathetic to the needs of parents. Teresa worked a part-time shift that allowed her to get out of work at three o'clock every day. Coupled with the flexibility of my own schedule (which was as flexible as one might expect while working at two jobs), we were able to make arrangements so that one of us was home on most days by the afternoon, reducing the need for daycare. Over the next few years, as our children began to attend school, our need to be home during the day was reduced even further.

This was how our lives went for the next three years. My medical practice continued to grow, and, despite the hassle of juggling a private practice and my hours at the hospital, I found the work quite satisfying. Teresa was also happy with her work at the army hospital. We were both employed in the field we'd spent years training (and then retraining) to be in. The prejudice we'd both encountered as medical residents was mostly behind us, as we'd earned the respect of both patients and fellow physicians through our hard work. And together we were making more money than we needed (even with four children).

Up until 1989, my practice was operated out of a rented space. But I felt it had grown enough that I could justify the cost of building a new office, something larger and better suited to the needs of a general medical practice. I'd discussed it with Teresa and found out that she was ready to leave the army hospital and start her own private practice as well. Eventually, we put together a plan for a dual office building, with one side dedicated to my practice and the other side dedicated to hers.

We wanted both the building and the property to belong to us, which meant applying for a mortgage at the bank. Getting the mortgage loan approved wasn't too difficult. We were both doctors, and my practice already gave me extensive ties within the community. The money would need to go toward more than just buying the property. There was the matter of hiring building contractors, purchasing building supplies, and applying for all the necessary permits to construct our medical office building.

The actual construction process took several months; in the meantime, both Teresa and I continued working at our jobs. At the same time, Teresa began laying out the groundwork for starting her own pediatric practice. Unlike my practice, which I'd been given by another doctor, she would essentially have to build hers from scratch. Again, most of the patients in any private practice come from referrals. While most of her patients at the army hospital weren't going to change practitioners, I was able to recommend her to patients of mine who had children.

By the time the new building was finished, Teresa already had enough patients to start her practice. In addition to bringing over my office manager to the new building, we hired a secretary to work for both of us. We each hired our own nurse to assist with patients. For many people, overseeing the construction of a new building and starting a private pediatric practice while raising four children would have been overwhelming, but Teresa never seemed to run out of energy. And as it turned out, she had one more massive task to handle. While the new building was still under construction, Teresa found out that she was pregnant once again. She wrapped up the year by giving birth to our fifth child, Angela, on December 20, 1989.

Chapter Fourteen

Isn't it funny how often a hobby can end up becoming more work than a regular job?

Shortly after moving to Elizabethtown, I began meeting with several other doctors and nurses for a morning run. I was well aware of the therapeutic benefits of regular running. Not only is it an excellent form of cardiovascular exercise, but the resultant endorphin rush is a great way to relieve stress naturally.

And make no mistake, running my own medical practice was stressful. Even a successful practice came with a lot of expenses. I not only had to secure new clients but also hold onto the ones I already had, challenging me to live up to the reputation of the man who'd founded the practice. I'd spent more than ten years working toward my own practice, and now that it was mine, the pressure to maintain it was overwhelming. On top of all that, at the end of every stressful day at the office, I would go home to a household that wasn't exactly relaxing. While my children were wonderful, there were five of them to look after and bring up.

So stress management was an issue for me. The situation was the same for the other members of my running group. We were all looking for a way to relieve stress and keep in shape. Whether you run a general practice or work in an emergency room, you all too often witness the effects of not staying in shape. Every day, we encountered heart conditions, joint damage, and other crippling effects of people eating the wrong foods and not getting enough regular exercise. And a doctor who's in poor physical shape won't inspire a lot of confidence in his patients.

We met at a fitness center between six and six thirty in the morning, then did our running together. The center had an indoor track, so neither rainy days nor other bad weather was ever an excuse to skip. After about an hour of running, we broke up to go to our respective jobs.

For a lot of people, daily running becomes a simple routine, like brushing their teeth. It's something they do because it has obvious health benefits and not doing it will lead to problems later in life. And for those people, simply running around a track at a fitness center is all they feel compelled to do.

But our running group was composed of medical professionals. And while not every medical professional is driven to excel in every activity, I've noticed that many people in that field have this urge to always take things to the next level. And, yes, we can be competitive. So it's not surprising that we began participating in running events.

Initially, these were just local events. We first entered the Louisville 5K Race. Like many such events, it was set up to benefit a charitable cause, and I was happy to help out. But there was definitely an appeal to matching myself against a larger group of runners. I'd already determined how well I could run when compared to the other people in my small group, but I was ready to compete against a much larger crowd; everyone in my group felt the same way.

After that first race, we began signing up for various others. The 5K races eventually gave way to 10K races, then to half marathons (21K or 13.1 miles), then to full marathons (42K or 26.2 miles). Participating in running events meant we had to spend more time running between those events. Our one-hour morning runs during the week would continue, but now we were also spending time training during the weekends as well. Many of these training sessions would be more than two hours, because the key to competing in a long-distance event is pacing and endurance rather than sheer speed. We were never sprinters.

Since a full marathon was so much longer than a 5K or 10K race, the training grew more intense over time. We would only participate in one or two marathons per year, but each one required three or four months of training beforehand. Eventually, we ran in marathons in Los Angeles, Chicago, and New York. We even participated in the Boston Marathon on three occasions.

While you've likely heard of the Boston Marathon, you might not know that it is the most prestigious marathon in the world, garnering the largest number of participants for such an event. It's also one of the largest spectator events in New England. And yet, for an event with so many participants, the event planners are quite selective in who they allow to participate. To qualify, I needed to fill out quite a bit of paperwork. Factors such as age, overall health, previous running experience, and even profession were taken into consideration. In many ways, it reminded me of the interview process I went through prior to entering the United States (or the various tests I had to pass before being allowed to practice medicine in this country). Like any other marathon, the Boston Marathon is an extreme endurance test, and people with health problems could seriously hurt themselves trying to run it. Not only did the event organizers want to make sure that nobody got hurt during the marathon, but they obviously wouldn't want to deal with any bad media coverage that came with someone getting seriously injured. Between my previous participation in other marathons, my excellent health, and the fact that I was a medical professional myself, I had no trouble demonstrating that I was physically capable of participating.

Between the daily commitment to running, the travel involved for participating in various events, and the expense (every event had an entry fee and I had to stay in a hotel before and after the event), I eventually met a limit to how far I could pursue this pastime. And while I still run regularly to this day, my marathon days are behind me. The last marathon I ran was the New York Marathon in 2005.

While Teresa was supportive of my running, she chose not to participate in my six o'clock fitness center sessions, nor in the marathons and other events that took me around the country. She found other ways to cope with the stress of raising five children while running her own medical practice.

One of the things that helped both of us cope with the stress of our family and respective practices was the fact that we weren't doing it alone. Once we were set up in the new building, we each had our own nurse. A secretary handled the appointments and incoming phone calls, and an office manager kept track of the budget and other day-to-day concerns of the business. All these people helped Teresa and me to focus on providing medical care rather than dealing with all the paperwork that accompanies such care. And for twelve years, we were fortunate enough to have hired a series of people who were both competent and dependable.

But things changed in 2003.

Chapter Fifteen

After the incident on United Airlines in 2017, a lot of people were suddenly very interested in my life. And thanks to the Internet, the people researching my background weren't limited to news reporters. But while the Internet is good at making information available to the public at large, it's bad at putting that information in context or vetting sources.

Which is to say that, if you did any online research about "David Dao," you might have run across references to my being arrested in 2003. While this is true, most of the other information you've read about my arrest is either false or taken out of context. When misinformation gets repeated enough times, people tend to assume that there must be some truth to it. And the Internet does a wonderful job of repeating misinformation through social media, reposting poorly researched articles and online journals citing those same articles without confirming any information. One of the reasons I've chosen to write this book is to tell the story about what happened before and after my arrest.

It began with a new office manager we hired in 2001. I'm going to refer to him as "BC." I first met BC as a patient in 2000. He'd been referred to me by another physician after he'd been complaining of chest pains. A year later, Teresa and I were looking for a new office manager, and because we were switching our files over to a new computer system, the ideal candidate needed a strong background in computers. While that may seem odd today, computers weren't quite as ubiquitous then as they are now; plenty of businesses still relied on paper records, and it wasn't safe to assume that a potential new employee was well-versed in using computers. Both Teresa and I had studied medicine when paper records were standard, so we were going through our own learning curves with modern technology and wouldn't be able to teach anyone else how to use the system.

Not only did BC have a strong background in computers, he also had a strong background in banking, which told us that he was trustworthy. If you've ever applied for a job at a bank (any job at any bank), you'll know that the background checks they conduct are among the most extensive for any line of work. So if he'd worked for a bank, we knew that someone had already vetted him.

As if his background in computers, his banking background, and the fact that I'd personally known him for a year weren't enough, he was also extremely active with his church; in fact, he was a youth minister. This was a man people trusted with the moral upbringing of their children. So it was probably safe to assume that Teresa and I could trust him to run our office.

As I mentioned earlier, in addition to my own medical practice, I also worked at Hardin Memorial Hospital. I usually started my days by making a daily round at the intensive care unit. Then, I drove to my office and took care of the patients in my own practice, returning to the hospital later in the day. I also spent time at home watching our children. Quite simply, I didn't have the time to keep an eye on my own office. My hours were split fairly evenly between my practice and the hospital, which meant that I needed an office manager I could trust. Teresa was also too busy to devote the time necessary to keep track of day-to-day paperwork.

Besides handling our financial accounts, a new office manager would have easy access to the private records of our patients, so it wasn't only our own information we were entrusting to him. Because trust was such an essential issue, Teresa and I both interviewed BC before deciding to hire him, even though I already knew him. The interview went smoothly; previous employers and his church spoke highly of him, and he had the professional skills required for the job. So there was no reason at the time for us to question our decision to hire him.

For the next year, things went well. To all appearances, BC was doing a fine job of managing our joint office. One of his responsibilities was to keep track of the billing for clients. While my wife trusted him, she liked to double-check the billing herself to make certain that no mistakes were made.

I'm not sure whether BC didn't realize that Teresa was double-checking the billing or if he thought she wouldn't catch the discrepancy, but, in 2002, she found that five thousand dollars had gone missing from our practice. This was the first time that she'd ever noticed such a discrepancy (with BC or any of the previous office managers). Once we confirmed that BC had stolen the money, we immediately fired him from our practice. At the time, we had no idea why he had stolen from us; in fact, neither of us cared about any reason he might have offered.

After letting BC go, we made a couple of calls. I contacted the police to let them know what had happened. Under Kentucky law, a five-thousand-dollar theft would have been classified as a Class D felony and carried a sentence of one to five years in prison. After I made the initial call to the police, Teresa took over the process of contacting our attorney and having charges officially brought against BC.

Teresa also called the church where BC worked as a youth minister to inform them of the situation. Since BC had stolen from us, there was no reason to believe that he wouldn't steal from his church as well. While this might seem spiteful, we truly were concerned about other people being victimized by this man. To be clear, my wife was only checking the accounts to make sure that BC hadn't made a mistake in the bookkeeping; neither of us had suspected that he would deliberately steal from us.

Shortly after contacting the police, we received a call from BC's father. He was in tears and begged us not to press charges against his son. He even agreed to pay back the five thousand dollars that his son had stolen.

Pursuing charges would have taken time that neither Teresa nor I were eager to give. There was no guarantee that BC would be found guilty, that a guilty verdict would include a fine, or that any such fine would even cover the stolen money. On top of all that, it was difficult to deny a father begging for his son's freedom, even if his son was guilty. For all those reasons, we chose to drop the charges.

Since we'd already warned the church about BC, we were fairly confident that they wouldn't be victimized in the same way. On top of that, any employer with whom he applied for work in the future would no doubt ask about our medical practice and his work as a youth minister; contacting us or the church would end with the story of his stealing money from us. So BC would suffer long-term consequences for what he'd done, even if he served no time in prison. It seemed like a fair punishment for a crime that wouldn't end up ruining a man's life, even though it certainly would make that life more difficult.

Looking back, dropping the charges was probably the biggest mistake I've ever made.

Chapter Sixteen

Once BC's father had paid back the money that his son had stolen, things began to settle back to normal for us. We hired a new office manager. While we had no reason to distrust BC's replacement, Teresa was even more careful when double-checking the expense records. Going through past records, she found no evidence that BC had ever taken any money from us before that point, which left us with the question of why he'd done so on this one occasion.

It would be three more months before I learned any more about what had happened. That was when BC called me. It was the first time that we'd spoken since Teresa and I had let him go. The first thing I did was ask him why he'd stolen from us. He explained that he was getting married and needed money for the wedding.

When Teresa and I had gotten married, years earlier, the ceremony had been remarkably simple. True, neither of us had family in the United States so the guest list was limited to a handful of friends, but I knew from personal experience that nobody "needed" thousands of dollars in order to get married.

On top of the question of why he thought he needed five thousand dollars was the question of why he thought we wouldn't notice the missing money. Initially, I'd assumed that he might not have realized that Teresa checked over our records, but the more I thought about it,

I realized that there was no way he couldn't have known that she did. He'd been our office manager for more than a year, after all.

While there was no excuse for what he'd done, BC did finally apologize for stealing from us. Apparently, he was still planning to get married. Whether his fiancée didn't care about the theft, forgave him for the theft, or somehow hadn't found out about the theft, I didn't bother to ask. He'd also found another job. Again, whether his new employer didn't care about his previous theft or didn't know about it was really none of my business (although no employer had contacted Teresa or me for a reference). So it seemed that, despite what had happened, BC was making an effort to turn his life around and had just called me to apologize.

A month after that phone call, I received another, far more frantic call from BC. This happened back in 2003, and I was not yet in the practice of carrying around a cell phone whenever I left the house. So when I say that he "called me," I mean that he paged me, and I called him back. Since he'd worked as my office manager, he knew my pager number.

When I called back, BC was crying. He'd lost his new job and needed money. I knew that the number I'd called wasn't BC's home phone, which led me to wonder if he was still living there…or if he had any home at all. Whatever the case, I decided that I'd heard enough and hung up the phone.

But he paged me again. And again. And again. I realized that the only way that I was going to get him to leave me alone was to talk with him. When I finally called him back again, I immediately made it clear that I wasn't going to give him any money.

BC then started telling me everything that had happened to him during the four weeks since I'd last spoken with him. In addition to losing his job, BC's fiancée had also left him; I didn't get an answer as to what specifically had caused her to leave him. The church where he'd served as a youth minister had let him go shortly after Teresa called them. After paying back the money that his son had stolen,

BC's father had disowned him as well. So BC had no job, no family, and not even the comfort of a religious community.

Then he told me that he didn't want to live any longer.

I wasn't BC's doctor. I certainly wasn't his friend. I honestly couldn't understand why, of all people, he would have called me for help.

On the other hand, I had known him for three years. If someone called you and said that he wanted to kill himself, would you turn your back on that person? Even if he'd lied to you and stolen from you? Could you hang up the phone? Could you bear to read a newspaper the next day and see a story about his taking his own life?

I wasn't a psychiatrist, but if BC was truly feeling as desperate as he sounded, I wanted to at least try to help him. At best, I might get him to go see an actual psychiatrist. Maybe he could move past what he'd done and make up for it by helping other people.

BC told me that he was staying at a hotel, which seemed odd until I thought about it. Maybe he'd been living with his fiancée and had to leave when she'd broken off their engagement. He couldn't stay with his parents, and most of his friends were probably part of the church that had severed ties with him. It struck me once again how absolutely alone this man must have been feeling at that moment.

So, I met with him and we spoke for a while. Again, he apologized for stealing from us, then he began going into further detail about how his life was coming apart. At no point did he ask for his old job back and there's no way I ever would have offered it to him. Besides the fact that we'd already hired another office manager, I knew that I would never be able to fully trust BC again. And even if I could trust him, Teresa would never allow him to work in the office that we shared. In fact, I hadn't even told Teresa that I would be meeting with BC, partially because I didn't think she'd understand how desperate he'd sounded on the phone.

During our conversation, BC once again asked me for money. Looking back, it was foolish, but after hearing what he'd been through, I wanted to help him, so I gave him two hundred dollars. Again, even though his problems were of his own making, I couldn't stand to see how bad off he was.

It was another six months before I spoke with BC again, in late July of 2003. Teresa and I had recently come back from a trip to New York when I got a call from our office manager (BC's replacement). She'd received a call from a pharmacist, claiming that somebody had tried purchasing drugs using my name. Apparently, something had seemed suspicious to the pharmacy staff and they'd decided to call my office to confirm the prescription. The office manager did a quick check and found no record that I'd written it. As soon as I realized that someone was attempting to use my identity to purchase drugs illegally, I immediately thought of BC.

Teresa and I had been so focused on reviewing our financial records to make sure that BC hadn't stolen any more money, neither of us had considered that he could have stolen anything else. In fact, purchasing drugs under my name was a much smarter plan than outright stealing money from my account; since he'd been the office manager, any questions about the drug purchases would have first gone through him, making it easy for him to cover things up. On top of that, purchasing drugs under my name and then reselling them wouldn't have resulted in any missing funds for Teresa to catch. If he hadn't stolen money from us, chances are that he could have continued with that plan indefinitely. And if he'd stopped doing it after getting fired, there was no way we ever would have discovered what had happened.

Like before when we'd caught him stealing from us, we contacted the police immediately to report that someone had tried to use my name to purchase drugs. This time we didn't have any evidence that it was BC who'd done it, but we did mention the fact that we'd fired him the year before for stealing five thousand dollars. We were assured that the police would look into it.

The following day, I received a call from BC. He didn't mention anything about drugs but said that he needed to see me. I asked him directly if he knew anything about illegally purchasing drugs under my name, but he said only that he would "explain everything when we get together." I didn't want to meet with him again, but he insisted that we meet and that he could only explain what had happened in person.

When we met at another hotel, BC sat at a small table and asked me to join him. I noticed that the bed had been made, which meant either that he'd just checked into the room or that he'd been there for several days and room service had already made the bed for that day. Still, there was noticeably no suitcase, scattered clothes, or other indications that he'd been in the room for any length of time. In fact, there seemed to be no sign that BC was staying in the room, almost as if he'd only rented it to meet with me.

Regardless, I sat across from BC, expecting him to ask for the money immediately. Instead, he pulled a bottle of pills out of his pocket and placed it on the table between us. I asked him, "What is this?"

Obviously, I knew that the bottle contained drugs. I didn't bother to pick up the bottle, much less open it, so I have no idea what sort of pills were inside. I assumed that these were some of the drugs that he'd purchased under my name. But why was he showing them to me?

BC simply pointed to the bottle. I wasn't sure what he was trying to do, but I had no interest in picking up the bottle. I tried to get him to tell me what had happened, reminded him that he'd promised to explain everything once we got together, but he said nothing, just looking from the bottle to me and back again. It felt as if he was waiting for something to happen or for me to do something about the pills on the table.

Finally, I was sick of waiting. I'd already contacted the police about the drug theft and mentioned BC's name to them. I'd certainly never asked him to purchase these drugs, so I couldn't figure out why he thought I'd want them. "I don't do drugs," I offered as an explanation, then moved away from the table.

At that point, the door to the hotel room was kicked in. Several plainclothes officers entered the room, and before I could process what was happening, I was told that I was under arrest for drug trafficking. I saw that BC was quickly pulled out of the room by some of those officers and realized that he'd been working with them.

Other than the fact that BC had worked with the police to get me arrested, I couldn't understand what had just happened. More than a decade later, I still have trouble understanding exactly what happened that night.

Chapter Seventeen

By the time I reached the police station, I had a rough idea of what had happened. After I had reported the prescription fraud to the police, they had apprehended BC. Rather than denying the crime, he'd chosen instead to make a deal with the police. He would offer testimony against his partner in this operation and, in exchange, he would receive immunity and all charges against him would be dropped. I was supposed to have been his "partner."

On a typical day, I would need to write several prescriptions for different patients. My usual practice was to write out these prescriptions and give them to the secretary at the end of each day. The secretary would then make certain that the patients got those prescriptions. From what I could gather, BC appeared to have taken some of those prescriptions off the secretary's desk, then had them filled, keeping the drugs for himself. Most of the prescriptions he took were for hydrocodone, OxyContin, and Percocet. He would then resell the drugs.

However, according to BC, he hadn't stolen anything from me. He alleged that we were partners and that I knowingly wrote false prescriptions for him (using the names of various patients as a cover) in exchange for sex and a portion of the drugs. I was charged with six counts of prescription fraud (for each of the patients whose names were on the prescriptions), as well as sixty-five counts of drug trafficking (for all the instances in which BC tried to get additional drugs without a signed prescription from me).

There were a lot of problems with his story. If I had been involved in a prescription fraud scheme, why would I have reported it to the police? In fact, if I'd been involved in illegal activities with BC for several years, why would I have reported his theft a year earlier? There was no rational reason why I would have reported crimes I'd helped commit, while BC had every reason to make up a story about my involvement in order to have the charges against him dropped. On top of that, I couldn't imagine that anything had happened at the motel room that would have convinced the police of my guilt.

When I arrived at the police station, I was surprised that I was first brought into a police detective's office rather than immediately placed in a cell. The detective took a few minutes to explain the charges to me, as well as the fact that BC had been working with the police to apprehend me.

At that point, I told him that I'd never had anything to do with drug trafficking. I hadn't known that any prescriptions had been taken until our current office manager, Sherry, had told me about the call she'd received from the pharmacy. I certainly wasn't committing prescription fraud. Not only that, but I'd essentially said the same thing to BC at the motel room, and, if he'd been wearing a wiretap, then the police would have heard me say it. So, I saw no reason why they would think I had committed any crime.

I was surprised that the first question the detective asked me wasn't about BC or prescriptions, but rather about how much money I made with my practice. Since I didn't keep track of my accounts, I could only give the detective a rough estimate. Teresa or Sherry could have given him a more precise number. BC could have probably given him a more precise number as well. After thinking on the number for a few seconds, the police detective told me that if I paid him $300,000, he wouldn't report me to the Kentucky Medical Board.

.It was clear that he wasn't discussing a fine or reparations for damages at this point. This was, plain and simple, a solicitation for a bribe.

I refused to pay the detective. At the time, I still believed that the simple fact that I had done nothing wrong would be enough to eventually get the charges dropped.

Once it was clear to the police detective that I wasn't going to give him any money, I was placed in a holding cell overnight. And while every police drama I'd ever seen on television said that anyone arrested was allowed to make a phone call, I was never given that opportunity.

In the morning, Teresa showed up and posted my bail. Since I hadn't been able to contact her, I didn't know how she'd even known that I'd been arrested. When I asked, she explained that the police had already been to our house and had spent several hours searching for drugs.

Once I was back home, I contacted my wife's church for help. While I didn't regularly attend services at St. James Church, the priest, Father Dick, knew me. Furthermore, he knew about BC and how he had stolen money from our practice the year before. Fortunately, Father Dick knew that one of his parishioners was an attorney and introduced me to him. Kenyon Meyer had ten years of experience, and, while he had an impressive record arguing cases before a jury, he tended to represent businesses rather than individuals, frequently litigating civil matters; criminal law was not the main specialty of his practice. Kenyon recommended that we hire a second attorney, Maury Kommor, as well. I had every reason to trust the legal advice of both these men.

But I couldn't understand how the prosecuting attorney planned to move forward with such a case. There were seventy-one charges being brought against me with absolutely no evidence of wrongdoing. In fact, the entire case seemed to hinge on a man with a criminal history who was offering his testimony simply to get the charges against him dropped.

In addition to our attorneys, my wife had a friend, Mildred Hubbard, who was willing to offer advice as well. While Mildred wasn't a lawyer herself, her husband was a prominent judge, and she had a surprising amount of insight into how the legal system worked. A few days after my arrest, I was contacted by the Kentucky Physician Health Organization and ordered to take a drug test. Mildred told me that taking such a test would be a good idea, since showing that there were no drugs in my system would go a long way toward disproving BC's claim that I was involved in a prescription fraud scheme in order to feed a drug habit.

The man who administered the drug test was one Dr. Brady. It was a straightforward test, administered in a lab of his choosing. I was confident that the drug test would help prove my innocence; unfortunately, I had forgotten to tell Dr. Brady that I was taking Ultram for some knee pain (related to my marathon running). Normally, I took ibuprofen, but that had begun to cause a stomach ulcer, so I'd gotten a prescription for Ultram. It was a minor dosage, but apparently enough to show up on a test. When Dr. Brady pointed out the positive result to me, I told him about my knee pain and showed him the prescription I had for Ultram. At the time, I thought that had settled the matter, but these results would come up later in court.

Unfortunately, my arrest and the charges against me had been picked up by local news media. It was covered in newspapers and on television. Not only did many of my patients hear about these charges, but many of my fellow physicians heard about them as well. This meant that both my private practice and my work at the hospital had to be suspended prior to the trial. I was technically "innocent until proven guilty," but I could tell that people were now suspicious of me.

Given that doctors are often called on to make life-and-death decisions and to defend those decisions if something goes wrong, professional ethics is a very serious matter. Not only would violating those ethics for personal gain be looked down on by other doctors, but any such violation would tend to make people more suspicious of any physician. So these sorts of charges didn't only harm the reputation of the doctor being accused, but that of doctors in general.

Shortly after my arrest, Kenyon and Maury convinced me to voluntarily give up my medical license. I thought once I'd had my day in court and been found not guilty, getting my license back would be easy. On the other hand, if I hadn't voluntarily given up my license, the Kentucky Medical Licensing Board might have had it suspended during the trial, and, even if I was found not guilty, having it reinstated would involve more work than if I'd simply done it of my own accord. Since I was no longer seeing patients anyway, I saw no harm in following my attorneys' advice.

The opinion of my attorneys would change six months later. At that point, we were still waiting for the case to go to trial. The prosecution had been working on the case and apparently had enough doubt over proving my guilt that they put together a plea bargain deal. Basically, they wanted me to plead guilty to only one count of prescription fraud. In exchange, all other charges against me would be dropped. Accepting the guilty plea would mean that my medical license would be suspended for two years, but it would also mean that I wouldn't be going to prison.

Kenyon and Maury both advised me to accept the plea bargain. But I refused. After all, I was innocent of any wrongdoing. Not only had I lost six months of my practice already to a false accusation, but BC was going to have all charges against him dropped because of that same accusation. Furthermore, once my license was reinstated, how many patients would I be able to attract to my practice when they learned that I'd confessed to writing fake prescriptions?

The fact that Kenyon and Maury wanted me to take the plea bargain told me that they either believed I was guilty or had no faith that they could defend me in court. So I fired them and hired two other attorneys. Mildred recommended Douglas Hubbard and Patrick Renn.

As it turned out, I had plenty of time to catch up on the details of my case, as it didn't go to court until almost a year after I hired them. Due to the nature of the case, I was charged with crimes in three different counties. I was charged in Hardin County (where I lived and where my practice was located), Nelson County (where BC lived), and Jefferson County (where the motel where I was arrested was located). Before any trial date was even set, the charges in Nelson County were dropped, leaving only two potential trials in my future and no strong assurance that I would win either one.

Chapter Eighteen

was arrested in July of 2003. My case didn't go to trial until
November of 2005. During that time, I wasn't practicing medicine.
Teresa was able to continue her practice without any trouble, and
I was still pulling income from a few properties that I'd purchased
over the years, so we weren't in any financial trouble. But it was
still difficult to cope with the fact that the career I'd worked so hard
to build for myself had been taken away overnight by a series of
false accusations.

Because of the media coverage during my initial arrest, as well
as the way so many of my fellow physicians had begun treating me,
I spent more time at home. But even at home, I couldn't escape
reminders of the trial, because I could tell that Teresa and my children
weren't entirely convinced of my innocence. It was nothing direct. No
one made accusations at the dinner table or anything like that. I just
had a sense that my family had begun keeping their distance from me.
And if my own family had trouble believing in my innocence, what
hope would I have in a courtroom? I felt isolated and depressed.

To make matters even worse, my attorney had advised me not to
speak about the case prior to the trial. This meant that, even if I did
meet with my patients, other doctors, or friends, I wouldn't be able to
discuss the one thing that they all wanted to ask me about. And when

I refused to discuss the case, I wondered if they took that to mean that I was guilty.

During this time, I'd begun attending church more often. My wife was Catholic, and she regularly took the children with her to St. James Church on Sundays. Besides the occasional service, I rarely joined them. But while I was waiting for my trial to begin, I started to look forward to those weekly gatherings. It was a chance to get out of the house, to surround myself with others without the pressures of having to make conversation. And I didn't have to worry about news reporters following me into the service to ask questions.

Even when I became a regular at Sunday services, I still wasn't baptized into the faith. Father Dick would frequently bring that up. After all, Teresa and our children had all been baptized. Why shouldn't I do the same?

I know the priest meant well. Despite not being a baptized Catholic, I was always made to feel welcome in the church (which was more important to me at that stage in my life than I think anyone realized). But I couldn't bring myself to go through with the ceremony. Quite simply, while I found the services to be comforting, I didn't believe in the power of Jesus Christ. I didn't have the faith of those around me and I didn't think it was right to pretend that I did. In my mind, being baptized when I didn't believe in Catholicism would be no different than lying.

Despite my nervousness, when the day of the trial finally arrived, I was relieved. I was informed that the prosecutors were still making their plea bargain deal available, but once again I rejected it. Both of my attorneys agreed with that decision, and that's one of the reasons why I chose to trust their advice. For example, they advised that both Teresa and I not take the stand. At first, I thought this was ridiculous. I'd done nothing wrong, so why wouldn't I want to speak in my own defense? Since no one in the world knew me better than my wife, why wouldn't I want her to speak in my defense as well? For that matter, why shouldn't we call in the six patients for whom I wrote those prescriptions, so they could testify that they had never received them?

My attorneys explained that even telling the truth, even confessing to no crime whatsoever, could backfire on me. Again, most of what I knew about courtroom proceedings came from what I'd seen on television. On television shows, guilty parties are often tricked by clever lawyers into giving away clues to their guilt. But as my attorneys made clear to me, in real life, innocent people often end up providing evidence in their testimony that gets them convicted. For example, a prosecutor might ask me if the prescription forms used had come from my practice or if the signatures on those forms were mine. By answering "yes" to both questions, I would be providing the prosecution with evidence to be used against me, despite not confessing to any crime. The same would go for Teresa.

Patrick went so far as to tell me that, if I did choose to testify, he would quit the case. He also advised against bringing up the police detective who'd asked me for $300,000. I couldn't understand how the detective asking for a bribe wasn't relevant. I was surprised to learn that this was actually a tactic sometimes used by the police to elicit confessions. Basically, under the pretense of asking for a bribe, the detective wanted to get me to confess to a crime. The idea was that an innocent man wouldn't pay to cover up a crime that he hadn't committed.

So the trial began with BC giving his testimony, no doubt rehearsed many times over the past two and a half years. Obviously, his immunity depended on that testimony, so he made it good. I knew firsthand how well he could win over somebody's trust, and I could tell that he was winning over the jury during my trial. And while I understood that testifying on my own behalf could backfire terribly, I still wondered if my silence made me look guilty to the jury. I'd spent months not speaking about this case with my friends and family, and I knew that they thought I was guilty. And now my silence might be condemning me in the eyes of these strangers as well.

After everything I'd gone through over the years, my career was being destroyed and I could only sit there and say nothing. I'd spoken up at the music conservatory back in Vietnam. I'd spoken up when I was in danger of losing my residency because I was "too foreign." Up until that trial, every victory I'd ever won in my life had come when I'd spoken against something that was wrong.

And now I was forced to be silent.

That trial went on for two weeks. The prosecution called in the police officers who'd arrested me, as well as the detective who had asked for a bribe. The only witness that my attorneys called was Sherry, my office manager, who had taken the initial calls from a pharmacist who was confused by one of BC's attempts to get prescription drugs using my name. She testified that I had told her to contact the police immediately when she brought it to my attention. She also testified that she knew that BC had a history of stealing from the medical practice, as well as drug dealing. I would have preferred having more people speak on my behalf, but I thought that her testimony did a lot to make my case.

Every day of the trial, I had to sit there, knowing that my wife didn't believe me, my children didn't believe me, my patients didn't believe me, and my fellow doctors didn't believe me. All of them had chosen the word of a known criminal over mine. To have twelve strangers on a jury doubt me didn't hurt nearly as much as to be doubted by the people I'd known for years, the people who meant the most to me.

The prosecution maintained that BC and I were partners in a prescription fraud and drug trafficking scheme. They alleged that I was a drug addict and cited the positive drug test result. They also alleged that I'd been arrested at the motel for purchasing a bottle of hydrocodone from BC.

Nothing about their case added up. According to their version of events, I had contacted the police to report that several prescriptions I'd written had been stolen. I'd even told them that I suspected

BC had stolen them. When BC contacted me the next day, I had repeatedly asked him if he had stolen prescriptions from me. When BC and I were together at the motel, I'd never even touched the bottle of pills and had certainly never handed over any money for them. The police had a recording of our meeting and, I presumed, the phone exchanges between us. Anyone reviewing those recordings would have seen that I never once suggested that there was a partnership between us. And I still couldn't understand why anyone would think that I'd not only turn in my partner if I was involved in a fraud scheme, but then try purchasing drugs from him the following day.

At this lowest point in my life (yes, even worse than what would happen years later on that airplane), I realized that I wasn't the only one who believed in my innocence. I had never been the only one who knew the truth. I had never been truly alone. I began to pray to God and Jesus Christ.

On the second-to-last day of my trial, after the lawyers had made their closing statements but before the jury had reached its verdict, I got in touch with Father Dick. That was the day I realized that I believed in God. That was the day that I chose to place my faith in Christ and be baptized into the Catholic Church.

Ordinarily, baptisms are large ceremonies. There is a mass, attended by the friends and family of the new member of the church. My baptism, by contrast, consisted of me and Father Dick. Even my family hadn't shown up, but that didn't matter. I wasn't getting baptized to prove anything to anyone, nor to make anyone else happy. I chose to be baptized to affirm what I believed to myself and God.

The following day, I arrived in the courtroom and waited for the jury's verdict. It took them an entire day to deliberate on the case. At first, I imagined they were debating my guilt or innocence, with passionate defenders on both sides (again, like on the television shows), but my attorneys explained to me that, in fact, they were probably taking so long because they had to reach an agreement on each of the seventy-one charges brought against me. Meaning that, even if they thought I was guilty (or not guilty) on all counts, they would still need to formally arrive at a separate verdict for each charge, one at a time.

After two and a half years of depression and isolation, the two weeks of the trial, and my recent conversion to Catholicism, it was hard for me to focus on anything. But I knew that, no matter what happened next, I'd done the right thing. I hadn't paid a bribe and I hadn't pleaded guilty to a crime I didn't commit. Despite the depression that had all but crippled me, I'd been able to discover a faith I might never have found if this hadn't happened.

When the jury returned, I was prepared for either verdict. Either I would be found guilty of drug trafficking and prescription fraud or I would be given my old life back. As it turned out, neither of those things occurred. On the sixty-five counts of drug trafficking, the jury found me not guilty. But on the six counts of prescription fraud, they found me guilty.

I was fifty-five years old and thought that my life was over. On that day, I would never have believed how much more I would still accomplish.

Chapter Nineteen

Before my trial, I never would have considered myself to be a Catholic. I wouldn't even have considered myself to be a spiritual or religious person. I believe I led a good life, supporting a family and helping people when I could. But once I was baptized into the Catholic Church, my view of the world and my place in it changed. I understood that everything happened for a reason. I had lost my name and my career, but I had found my faith in God and felt at peace. I don't believe it's possible to understand why I made the decisions I made after the trial without explaining my views on religion.

As a child, I was raised in a Buddhist household. I'm not the first one to point out the similarities between Christianity and Buddhism. There is, in fact, a school of thought that asserts Jesus himself was exposed to Buddhism before beginning his own ministry (since Buddhism predates Christianity by six centuries).

One similarity between the two religions is in the messengers themselves. Both Jesus and Buddha were poor in material wealth. While Jesus was born to humble means, Buddha was born into a wealthy family but gave up his wealth. Neither man needed wealth to preach his message. From a professional standpoint, both of these men would have been considered "failures" in modern society because they didn't have respectable careers or a lot of money. Having recently lost my practice, there was an appeal to someone who could win respect despite not having a successful career.

Jesus spent his later years helping the sick and the poor, especially those who were looked down upon by society. Criminals, foreigners, and the terminally ill…the Bible had stories of Jesus interacting with all these outcasts. Buddha also framed his moral lessons as being applicable to all people, not simply the wealthy or the powerful or the respected. In fact, both Jesus and Buddha became outcasts themselves in their respective struggles to speak the truth. It was almost as if one had to become an outcast in order to truly see what mattered in this world.

The chief difference I saw between Jesus and Buddha was in their teachings on sin. Buddha's role was much more that of a teacher than a savior; he would offer a moral lesson and provide people with the means to save themselves from sin, but not require people to confess or otherwise take responsibility for their actions. With Jesus, on the other hand, there was a more lasting connection. This was not a man who simply taught right from wrong, then sent you on your way. Once I was baptized into the Catholic Church, I accepted that Jesus would be a partner in my life, walking beside me and continuing to guide my actions throughout my life.

I understand that many of the people reading my story won't share my religious beliefs. And I wanted to compare Jesus with Buddha not to show that one was better than the other, but to show that their similarities far outnumber their differences. For those who practice any other faith, the same holds true. I don't believe that religion is meant as a way to answer questions about the universe (where the universe came from or what happens after we die), but rather a blueprint for behavior.

So I had accepted Catholicism as my blueprint for behavior. What did that mean? Jesus was a healer and a teacher. He never discriminated against rich or poor, reaching out to tax collectors and street beggars alike. At the same time, much of his work focused on the poor simply because they needed more help than the rich. He did it without money. And he did it even when people spoke ill of him.

I'd been a teacher; in my own way, I'd also been a healer. While I was on probation, I had no license to practice medicine. Recertifying as a teacher would also be next to impossible, given my criminal record. But I still had the skills for teaching and treating the sick.

I wanted to help the poor, as Jesus had done. I had a wife and children to consider as well; I wasn't going to abandon my family to help strangers. But I truly believed that, if I maintained my desire to help others, God would provide me with an opportunity, license or no license.

In the meantime, I waited.

Chapter Twenty

The good news was that the drug trafficking charges against me had been dropped. If convicted of drug trafficking, I could have been sentenced to decades in prison (which at my age would have effectively been a life sentence). Instead, I'd only been convicted of prescription fraud, which brought a sentence of five years' probation. I would be required to submit to a weekly drug test, but I would not be going to prison. In addition, once the Jefferson County court system learned about the verdict in the Hardin County court, they dropped their charges against me, meaning that I wouldn't have to be tried again for the same allegations. Unfortunately, my career was effectively on hold during the probation period. And once the five years were finished (at which point I would be sixty-three years old), I would have to go through an extensive process to get my medical license back.

Teresa was still practicing medicine, but we had five children to support, and even her thriving medical practice wouldn't be enough to cover our expenses. Since our children were now attending college (with some even beginning their work on advanced degrees), our financial burden had grown even heavier. Practicing medicine and teaching were no longer open to me as career options, so I had to contribute in some other way.

I'd begun investing in rental properties several years earlier. Originally, I'd been interested in property ownership mostly for the lucrative tax deductions that were possible. But as I'd grown older, I saw them as a sort of retirement plan. Stocks would rise and fall, but rental properties would provide me with a steady passive income every month, no matter how well or poorly our other investments did.

Only one of the rental properties I owned was in Louisville. All the others were out of state. This meant that, while I was active in monitoring the one local property, all the others were managed by a firm I'd contracted. So managing my various properties still didn't account for much of my time.

I had once told Teresa half-jokingly that the rental properties would take care of her if anything ever happened to me. At the time, I'd imagined a health problem or accident ending my medical career. I'd never thought that my license would be taken from me due to a criminal conviction. But while my probation prevented me from getting a job as a teacher or a doctor, having a criminal record didn't prevent me from being a landlord. The rental properties turned out to be a good idea and helped round out our family finances so that we could comfortably meet our obligations.

Chapter Twenty-One

After I voluntarily gave up my medical license in 2003, I had a lot of free time on my hands. And with my increased isolation from friends and professional associates, I found myself spending a lot of time at home with nothing to do. This is when I began watching more television.

Some of my favorite programs were cooking shows. Before meeting Teresa, I'd spent several years living on my own and had become quite a good cook. In the past, I'd told people that I wanted to become a professional chef one day, but I'd never meant it as more than a joke. After all, a chef needed to attend school to train in the culinary arts. On top of that, I loved being a doctor and would never have seriously considered giving up that career to be a chef.

But as I watched one cooking show after another, I realized that I had the time, the money, and the desire to pursue this completely different career path. And I needed to do something with my time for at least the next two years. So I enrolled in the culinary arts program at Sullivan University in early 2005 and began classes that fall.

Ordinarily, I would have discussed this sort of career shift with my wife prior to enrolling in classes, but Teresa still wasn't speaking with me. At that point, she still believed that I had been involved in a prescription fraud scheme with BC, and I honestly don't know whether a not-guilty verdict on all the charges would have changed her opinion. For that matter, I had no idea how my children, patients, or fellow doctors would have felt if the verdict had been different. In a way, I wanted to go back to school not only to learn a new skill, but also to cultivate new friendships with people whose opinion of me hadn't been changed by the trial.

Given my medical background (especially my surgical work), I picked up cutting and knife skills quite easily. I had plenty of practice holding a blade steady in my hand. And after all the medical terminology I'd needed to memorize, recipes were easy to remember.

But my background in music was what I feel helped me the most in studying culinary arts. Cooking is far more like an art form than a science. You need to be precise (both in cutting and measuring), but you also need a passion to create something new. As I continued with my studies, I found that each chef produced meals that were uniquely his or her own. Think of it like a dozen blues musicians all playing the same standard: the notes are always arranged in the same order, but each musician produces a version that no one else can duplicate.

Besides my background in medicine and music, it turned out that my background in marathon running also helped me become a better chef. At fifty-six, I was at least twice as old as most of the other students in the program. I'm sure being older would intimidate many returning students, but I enjoyed the sense of competition. These were just cooking classes and I wasn't actually competing against anyone. We were all there to learn. But when you're in your fifties and surrounded by people in their twenties, you can't help but notice all the ways they underestimate you. It was nothing overt, but I could see that my classmates (and even some of my instructors) expected me to be slower, clumsier, and maybe even more forgetful than the younger students. I experienced more than a little satisfaction in seeing their surprise when I proved more capable in the kitchen than they'd assumed.

While I'd hoped to make new friends at school, the fact that most of my classmates were half my age made it difficult. Besides, I was never sure which of them knew about the charges that had been brought against me. While mine was not a household name, anyone doing a Google search would have found multiple articles concerning my arrest and trial; I therefore found myself constantly second-guessing things that were said to me and overanalyzing people's facial expressions when they spoke with me. Who knew? What did they know? What did they believe? Despite having avoided prison, I found myself isolated from other people, even when I was in a classroom with thirty other students.

After a year of courses, I graduated from Sullivan University's culinary arts program. Shortly after that, I got a position as a chef at Winston's Restaurant. The restaurant was largely staffed by students and graduates from Sullivan University and served mostly gourmet American cuisine. Like the cooking classes, working in a restaurant was challenging but also interesting. Again, I was starting out at age fifty-eight in this field, while most of the other beginning chefs were in their middle twenties.

Unfortunately, my cooking career was cut short after only three months. The kitchen was broken down into different stations, each specializing in a particular type of dish. In some ways, it was like working in a hospital, where everyone had the same basic medical training, but we each had our own specialty as well. One night, I was assigned to the sauté station, where I'd never previously worked. Sauté work requires the frequent use of both hands and a lot of coordination. My grip on one of the sauté pans slipped, and I ended up burning my hand rather badly. While there was no permanent damage or scarring to my hand, the experience was extremely painful, and I couldn't work in the kitchen for several days afterward. While I was at home letting my hand heal, I realized that I wasn't truly satisfied with this work and wanted to move on, so I tendered my resignation without ever returning there.

Since then, the only person I cook for is my wife.

Chapter Twenty-Two

By the end of 2006, I'd applied for and completed a culinary arts program, gotten a job as a chef, and injured myself badly enough that I had quit. I still wasn't able to get my medical license back, and, even after my probation was over, I would need to go through a lengthy process before I could practice medicine again. All of which is to say that, after I burned my hand, I was back home and watching television again.

This time, I became fascinated with televised poker tournaments. While many of these tournaments were essentially charity events with celebrity players, I also saw many professional poker players, men and women, who treated the game like any other professional sport. I'd never played the game in my younger days, but I decided to buy a book and teach myself the rules.

Shortly after learning the rules, I began going to local casinos and playing poker for single-dollar bets. I wasn't trying to earn any money, I was simply learning the game and mastering some new skills. Succeeding at poker required a combination of the ability to read people, mathematics, and luck. As a doctor, I had extensive experience "reading" people, determining when they were being honest with me and when they were holding something back. Ask any musician about mathematics and they'll tell you that recognizing patterns is one of the keys to composing great music. And as for luck...mine ranged from the very good (how I met my wife) to the very bad (how I lost my medical career). Unfortunately, luck was the one thing that I couldn't learn, but I could use certain strategies to minimize my risks so that I'd depend more on the people reading and math skills and less on luck.

At first, Teresa was concerned about the time I was spending at the casinos. While we were doing well financially, she knew that gambling could ruin people's lives if it got out of hand. On more than one occasion, she told me that she was worried that I might develop a gambling addiction. I could see exactly how my new interest might appear from her point of view. I'd been spending a lot of time at home, isolated from other people, watching television, and now I'd taken up gambling. At this point, I was still submitting to a weekly drug test, so addiction was certainly on my wife's mind. I could only assure her that I was playing for such low stakes (single-dollar bets) that there was no way poker could ruin us financially.

Teresa's fears grew stronger when I began entering poker tournaments. These games required a buy-in of fifty or a hundred dollars. The stakes grew, but so did the payouts. I began winning enough money that I had to report it on my taxes. I still lost games from time to time (nobody wins all the time), but I generally won more money than I lost. And once Teresa saw that I was making a profit from gambling, she ceased to worry.

Eventually, I worked my way up to the World Series of Poker annual competition in Las Vegas. These tournaments ordinarily run from a couple of days to two or three weeks and involve more pacing than luck. In many ways, it was similar to the reality show *Survivor*, where players get winnowed away in the early rounds until only a handful of them remain at the end. It was also like the marathons that I'd run years earlier. I couldn't count on an unbroken streak of luck to carry me through, so instead, I chose to pace myself over multiple rounds. While I didn't win first place in that competition, I did return to Louisville with more than a hundred thousand dollars in winnings.

Since then, I've played in several poker tournaments, large and small, and have made close to half a million dollars total over the years. Besides the money, playing poker helped me deal with my depression. It got me out of the house as I traveled to various competitions. It gave me a way to use the various skills I'd learned over a lifetime. And it gave me the opportunity to win once in a while—which isn't too bad for someone who didn't even know how to play the game before age fifty-five.

But eventually, I needed to do more than just get out of the house and make money. I was still attending church regularly and still felt a need to help other people. And while cooking and gambling were diversions that kept my mind active and earned me some money, those things weren't making anyone's life better. After being drug-free for two years (as confirmed by my weekly drug tests), my probation was reviewed and reduced from five years to only two, meaning that my probation was finished three years early. I was now able to start the lengthy process of getting my medical license reinstated.

But as it turned out, someone needed my help immediately.

Chapter Twenty-Three

I haven't mentioned what my parents were doing during my time in the United States. I was able to get back in touch with them shortly after I'd arrived here in the mid-1970s. Unfortunately, communication technology wasn't what it is today. There was no Internet, and telephones weren't as common in Vietnam as they are today. Neither of my parents was able to afford a telephone, and, even if either of them had the money to purchase one, they didn't live in areas of the country where phone service was available. What this meant was that, for about twenty years, we communicated exclusively through letters in the mail.

Like so many immigrants before me, I sent money to my parents whenever my earnings from my work allowed for it. As my medical practice (as well as my investments) grew more profitable, I sent more money. In the late 1990s, I was able to send enough money to my father to have a phone installed in his home.

Unfortunately, by that point, my mother had passed away, so I was never able to speak with her again after I left Vietnam. She had been a huge influence on my life in ways that she probably never realized. Like me, she'd had a passion for cooking. And after her divorce, she began a clothing design business, starting over in much the same way that I'd had to start over in a new career after my conviction. I would have loved to have spoken with her again and let her know how much her life inspired me to try new things and not let setbacks ruin my life. But all I could do was try to help the people who were still alive.

I returned to Vietnam twenty-five years after I'd left.

By the start of the twenty-first century, the political situation had changed enough that I wasn't afraid of running into trouble with the government if I went to Vietnam. I was also able to afford the trip, but my medical practice and my family took up all my time, and I simply couldn't justify traveling to my homeland.

It wasn't until 2000 that I took time away from my practice to visit after I received a call from my brother. Our father was having serious health issues and needed to see a doctor. Unfortunately, he was eighty-seven years old at the time and not wealthy enough to get the local physicians to see him.

I should probably explain some of the differences in how medicine was practiced in Vietnam as opposed to the United States. Since the fall of Saigon in 1975 (and Teresa's escape from Vietnam in 1980), some things had changed in how medicine was practiced. Vietnamese doctors kept themselves informed on medical breakthroughs, but quality medical care was still something of a luxury reserved only for those who could afford it.

In Vietnam, a patient was expected to pay both the doctor and the nurse up front before any treatment was begun. In fact, the treatment would often begin before a full checkup and diagnosis were made, meaning that many patients would end up paying for treatments that they didn't even need. Since the public still had great respect for medical professionals' authority, patients rarely questioned what doctors told them, and getting a second opinion was unheard of (not to mention prohibitively expensive).

It was therefore safer and less expensive for me to go to Vietnam and perform an evaluation. Given my background in pulmonary medicine, I felt that I could properly diagnose any heart problems my father might be having. I even brought an EKG machine with me, since I doubted I'd be given access to medical equipment.

When I saw my father again, I found that he was living in a mobile home with my brother. The two of them ran a small shop that sold rice. While I knew that the money I sent to my father wasn't making him wealthy, I was still shocked to see how he was living.

After finishing my examination, I concluded that he was suffering from a heart blockage and needed to have a pacemaker installed. Fortunately, I still had old friends from medical school who remembered me and were willing to help when I called. One of those friends had become a hospital director and made a room available for me to perform my father's operation; he even assisted me during the surgery. Together, we implanted the pacemaker without any trouble.

Since I still had a medical practice at that time, I couldn't stay in Vietnam for longer than a week. A year later, I got another call about my father. The pacemaker I'd installed needed to have the battery replaced, and, once again, he couldn't afford to have any of the local physicians perform the operation. Again, I went to Vietnam, and again the surgery to replace the pacemaker battery was straightforward and free of complications.

But while my father's heart problems were relatively easy to repair, his financial difficulties would take considerably more work. Fortunately, the money I'd earned in the United States went a lot further in Vietnam, and I was not only able to purchase some land, but the three-story house I built there for my father and brother to live in was an improvement over the mobile home in every way. I also had a second three-story house built so my father could rent it out to someone else and use the money to better support himself. After all, I'd learned firsthand how property management could support a man when he wasn't able to continue working.

While it took six months to complete construction on the two houses, I was only in Vietnam for two weeks. The money I'd been sending helped, and I could see that my brother was able to handle my father's day-to-day needs without me. Once the surgery had been performed, there wasn't much I could do for him.

I'd replaced the pacemaker battery in 2002 and had then been arrested for prescription fraud in 2003. For the next two and a half years, I spent a great deal of time and effort in preparing for my trial. After being convicted in late 2005, I was placed on probation, which prevented me from leaving the country.

My father knew all about the criminal charges that had been brought against me, but since he was only hearing about these charges from me and not the television and newspaper reports, he wasn't swayed by the various false stories out there.

I didn't return to Vietnam until 2009. When I arrived, I clearly recognized that my father's health had taken a sharp decline and that he wasn't going to live for much longer. And while my brother was still taking care of him from day to day and the second house was providing enough money for the two of them to live comfortably, I chose to stay in Vietnam to be with my father for whatever time he had left. Without a medical practice, the choice was easier.

I explained the situation to Teresa over the phone, and, while she was worried for my safety, she understood why I needed to stay there. Since she had been in Vietnam for several years after the fall of Saigon, her memories of the country were far darker than my own. Despite everything that had happened over the last few years, I knew that she still loved me, and I made a point to call her frequently.

When my father's stomach began bleeding, I could do nothing more for him, and he died peacefully in his home, just like he wanted. Once he was cremated, nothing else kept me in Vietnam. My brother stayed in my father's home and continued to earn an income from the second house as well as the rice shop. I was no longer needed.

When I returned to the United States, I was still dealing with the loss of my father, but I was also dealing with the fact that I no longer had anything to do. Poker tournaments and property management brought in money, but I needed to do more than just make money. My father's pacemaker surgery and battery replacement were the only medicine I'd practiced in five years. And even with my probation finished, I had no idea how long it would be before I could practice medicine again. I prayed to God for guidance on what I should do next with my life.

My prayers were answered three months later with an unexpected job offer. Doctor Hai was another friend that I'd made decades earlier while I was studying medicine. The specific job he offered me was setting up an intensive care unit (ICU) in a hospital in Vietnam and acting as its director. The salary was generous (roughly two thousand dollars a month when converted to American currency). In addition to the salary, I would also be offered room and board at the hospital.

Doctor Hai understood that if I was going to set up and run an ICU, then I would run it the way I thought a medical ward should be run. Incoming patients would not be required to pay up front before they received medical treatment. And no treatment would be given before a doctor (often myself) first spoke with them about their symptoms. While this system of medical treatment wasn't initially as lucrative as the established system of Vietnamese medicine, we soon discovered that patients were traveling great distances to be treated at our hospital rather than consulting with their local physicians. Treating patients with greater respect often resulted in more accurate diagnoses and thus more effective treatments.

Eventually, our ICU began hiring other doctors, and I trained them in this different method of medical treatment. While they enjoyed a similar success rate to my own, I found that many other physicians didn't appreciate what I was doing. They were concerned that their careers were in danger as patients began to leave their practices. In their view, I was practicing "American" medicine, using American medical terminology and American medical customs. While I'd initially learned those American medical terms in a Vietnamese medical school, that had been before the fall of Saigon and the purging of all Western influences.

In many ways, the old method of treatment was closer to what one might expect from a veterinarian treating a dog rather than from one human being giving another human being health care. What I was doing was not only training doctors to be better at their jobs, but also training patients to value their own observations. Many physicians didn't like the fact that this new method meant that patients looked at them with less awe. Medical advice was regarded less as sacred writ and more as the insight of a trained professional, similar to a mechanic offering an opinion on a faulty engine.

Another factor in how doctors were treated differently in the United States than in Vietnam had to do with the process of medical licensing. In the United States, medical licenses needed to be renewed on an annual basis, meaning that doctors had to constantly retrain and uphold certain medical standards or risk losing their licenses. In Vietnam, medical licenses were generally issued for life, and, while there was certainly conduct that would result in a doctor's license being revoked, it rarely happened. This resulted in Vietnamese doctors feeling far more secure in their positions and far more likely to do things "their way" instead of in a way that was better for their patients.

I have the greatest respect for Vietnamese physicians. Many of them have to work with fewer resources than what was available to me in the United States. They don't communicate as freely with one another, meaning that each of them has to develop his or her own signature approach to medicine. And many of them work in impoverished parts of the country, meaning that they often can't make enough money to cover their expenses (which is likely one of the reasons that so many have adopted a "pay up front" model of business).

But I had the means and the opportunity to provide a different type of medical service, and I made the most of it. While I never spoke about my religious beliefs at the hospital, I like to think that my work put those beliefs into action. I even prayed before meeting each of my patients. And I truly believe that my success at the medical ward was due to a combination of treating patients with greater respect and trusting in God to guide my decisions. Some of these successes were almost miraculous, as we had more than one patient brought to us who had been declared dead by another physician, only to be revived by the doctors at our ICU.

I believe that, if you're going to help people, then you should do it to the best of your ability. And while various denominations of Christianity have turned away people for their gender, their race, or their sexual preference, Jesus himself offered his teachings to all people; so I wanted to set up a medical ward that would accept all people, regardless of their income or political affiliation. Even if none of the doctors I trained considered themselves to be Christian, I believe that they all practiced the best parts of Christ's teachings.

Once I had trained the doctors in the medical ward and this different system of treating patients had begun to gain popularity, I was ready to return to the United States. It was time for me to begin work on getting my medical license back.

Chapter Twenty-Four

I mentioned that my probation was reduced to two years, thanks mostly to the consistently negative results from my weekly drug tests. Unfortunately, my medical license wasn't automatically reinstated once my probation was finished. In fact, the process of getting my license back lasted longer than my original probation period of five years.

One of the reasons for the lengthy delay had to do with my father's illness. While I was in Vietnam, I wasn't able to begin work on getting my license back. It is a bit ironic that one of the reasons I couldn't regain my license to practice medicine in the United States was because I was running an intensive care unit in Vietnam. I'd learned back in 1975 that earning a medical degree in Vietnam didn't mean that I had the right to practice medicine in the United States (just as having that license revoked in the United States didn't affect my ability to practice medicine in Vietnam).

So, despite having applied to have my license reinstated back in 2007, my trips to Vietnam meant that the process couldn't begin until I was back in the United States in 2010. But before my application could go forward, the Kentucky Health Organization required that I undergo a lengthy psychological examination. My initial evaluation took place at a treatment center in Pennsylvania and lasted several days. Once that was finished, I was sent to Pine Grove, a facility in Mississippi, for a more extensive series of tests.

At this point, you might be curious why I had to undergo so much testing before having my medical license reinstated. After all, the only crime I'd been convicted of was prescription fraud. While it would certainly be unethical to sell prescriptions, there was nothing to suggest a psychological disorder. However, given the positive result on my drug test (due to the prescribed pain medication I was taking at the time), as well as the specific charge that I'd traded prescriptions for sex, it was the opinion of the Kentucky Health Organization that I might be suffering from a drug and/or sex addiction.

Pine Grove Behavioral Health and Addiction Services specializes in treating people who suffer from various types of addiction. It's what you might consider a "high end" clinic, the sort of place where celebrities go for treatment. And in fact, I met my share of lawyers, CEOs, and even other doctors while I was there.

During my first four weeks at the facility, my day was broken down into a morning meditation, a meeting with a doctor, time at the gym in the afternoon, and several classes. I was paying quite a bit of money for my stay, and I could leave any time I wanted. But leaving before this evaluation was complete would mean that I could never practice medicine in the United States again. So, in many ways, I felt like a prisoner.

After my first four weeks at Pine Grove were finished, I needed to return for an appointment once every three months. In addition to these visits, I was to see a psychiatrist in Louisville once a week. This period reminded me of my probation experience, with a weekly check-in, followed by a longer appointment every few months, but with a treatment facility instead of a court. While all of this was happening, I had to deal with the fact that my wife and children, unable to manage the stress and the dark thoughts occasioned by this situation, sometimes questioned my innocence. I was severely anxious over what lay ahead in my future. I was no longer in any danger of serving prison time, but my work in Vietnam had left me eager to begin practicing medicine in the United States again.

I still owned multiple properties that brought in a passive income while I was waiting for my evaluation results. I was also in contact with a lawyer in Vietnam about some other properties. After my father died, there was some dispute concerning who should inherit his two houses. And much like getting my medical license reinstated, settling the inheritance dispute was a lengthy process. In fact, I didn't gain settled ownership of those properties until 2011.

Finally, after two years of weekly evaluations and occasional trips to Pine Grove, the results of my extensive testing were ready. First, the various psychiatrists who'd interviewed me all confirmed that I was neither a drug addict nor a sex addict. However, they did diagnose me with four psychological conditions and a health issue: I was diagnosed with post-traumatic stress disorder, dependent personality disorder, depression, and anxiety disorder. They also determined that I was diabetic. Despite my frustration over this entire process, I could understand how they'd reached these conclusions.

Most people hearing about post-traumatic stress disorder (PTSD) normally associate it with veterans returning from a war. I knew that a significant number of soldiers who'd served during the Vietnam War had been diagnosed with this disorder, but although I had been a member of the armed forces during that conflict as well, my service had not placed me directly in any combat role. At the time I was diagnosed, the Vietnam War was thirty-five years past, and I wondered how long I'd been suffering from this condition without thinking that it was anything unusual. I felt occasional heightened amounts of stress; I had vivid recollections of fleeing Vietnam; I sometimes had trouble concentrating. I had simply never considered these things to be symptoms of a medical condition.

And even if I hadn't gone through the stress of fleeing Vietnam, there was also the matter of my parents' divorce. I had never forgotten what had happened all those years ago, and when I'd returned to visit my father, the subject had never come up. He was very sick, after all, and I hadn't wanted to upset him. On top of that, my mother had already passed away, so there seemed to be no point in getting him to apologize for what he'd done to her. But being in Vietnam for ten months, surrounded by so many reminders of my childhood, had resulted in my repeatedly reliving many of those traumatic events.

My father had left my mother because he thought she'd had an affair. He was no longer able to trust her, no matter what she said to him. I suppose there was more than a passing similarity to my own marriage. While I'd never had an affair and Teresa never accused me of such a thing, she certainly had trouble trusting me after the trial. I found that there was nothing I could say or do to get my wife (or my children or most of my friends) to trust me again.

The diagnosis of dependent personality disorder was a bit more difficult for me to understand. This disorder is defined by a strong fear of separation. People with this condition tend to be "clingy" in relationships. If anything, I felt that I had spent a great deal of time separated from my wife, both when I was pursuing interests such as marathon running and tournament poker playing and when I spent close to a year in Vietnam to help my elderly father and establish a medical ward. At the same time, this disorder is often defined by extreme narcissism and a desire to control various situations. While I didn't feel as if I was in control of much of my life, I could certainly agree that I had a desire for greater control.

Depression was probably the easiest of the diagnoses for me to accept. I knew that I was depressed. I could also argue that I had several good reasons for that depression: losing my medical practice, being convicted of a crime I hadn't committed, not being trusted by the people closest to me...and the death of my parents. I could make the argument that anyone who didn't feel depressed under those circumstances might well be suffering from some other psychological condition. On the flip side, I believe that I was already handling that depression quite well before this diagnosis, mostly by trying to fill my days with new activities. I was also trying to focus my efforts on helping others rather than brooding on my own misfortunes.

The anxiety disorder, like depression, seemed less like a psychological problem and more like a logical reaction to my situation. I felt worried most of the time. I had no idea what was going to happen in my future.

And then there was the diabetes, which was in many ways the easiest condition to treat. The treatment entailed a restricted diet, some medication, and regular exercise.

After all the testing was finished, I was told only that I could now begin the process of reapplying for my medical license. The two years of testing had only been the first step.

Chapter Twenty-Five

Before approaching the Kentucky Medical Board to get my medical license back, I thought it would be a good idea to hire an attorney to help me through the process. The man I hired, Chad Elder, seemed ideal for the job. I'd first heard about him during my initial trial back in 2003. I knew that he'd worked for the board before switching over to a private practice. In fact, his specialty was medical licensing. After all the work I'd had to do during my evaluations at Pine Grove, it was nice to have someone helping me through the process.

Unfortunately, Chad immediately handed my case off to his partner. But his partner didn't know nearly as much about the medical licensing process as Chad did. After nine months spent going back and forth with the board (and eight thousand dollars in legal fees), they asked me who would be acting as my preceptor. This was the first time that I'd thought I would need a preceptor, and Chad's partner seemed to be taken off guard by what I would later learn was a standard part of this process.

A preceptor is a doctor who acts as a mentor to a physician in the process of being reinstated. The preceptor would show me how to behave properly around patients, then monitor my work to make sure I didn't do anything wrong. I was sixty-six years old at this point and had been practicing medicine on and off for forty years, but now I was told that I needed a mentor to monitor my work. And since acting as a preceptor required a lot of time and effort, finding one wasn't going to be easy.

Finding out that I needed a preceptor essentially caused the whole process to start over again. I let Chad's partner go as my attorney. For a brief time, I was so sick of lawyers that I thought it would be easier to simply represent myself. Without going into any embarrassing details, I'll just say that it quickly became apparent that I was not able to adequately represent myself. I eventually hired Clay Wortham, an attorney who was able to help me through the medical licensing process without any difficulty.

The next step in the process was to go through an evaluation at the Center for Personalized Education for Physicians (CPEP) in Denver, Colorado. CPEP is a nonprofit organization that, among other things, evaluates physicians for competence. By this time, it was 2015, twelve years since my arrest and twelve years since I'd given up my practice. Even though I'd practiced medicine since then in Vietnam, that wouldn't count toward regaining my license to practice medicine in the United States. From their point of view, I hadn't practiced medicine in more than a decade, so it made sense that someone should confirm that I was still able to do so. On the other hand, the length of this evaluation process eventually went from the inconvenient to the unreasonable.

The initial CPEP evaluation involved two days of testing at the Denver facility and cost six thousand dollars (plus the expense of a hotel and travel). This testing focused on my understanding of pulmonary medicine. I still have no idea why it would cost thousands of dollars to check the answers on a test.

I passed this initial evaluation test with no trouble. Why wouldn't I? One of my specialties was pulmonary medicine. The crime I'd been convicted of was one of ethics, not negligence. There was no malpractice suit against me, and I had already passed an extensive neuro-psychosexual evaluation from Pine Grove. There was nothing in my background to suggest that I wasn't competent to practice medicine.

I sometimes remember my residency training and how I was almost cut from the program due to an alleged "language barrier." As I went through this ridiculous evaluation process, I couldn't help but wonder if my ethnicity played a role in so many people questioning my competence to practice medicine once again.

After passing that initial evaluation, I was required to study medicine for the next three months. The studying was largely independent, but I would be tested to confirm that I understood the basics of medicine. Every stage of this studying process carried with it a price tag. So perhaps these tests weren't a matter of people questioning my competence, but rather just an easy way to make money by administering unnecessary tests. I was fortunate in that I had other means of income besides my medical practice. I can't imagine how anyone who relied solely on a medical practice for money would have been able to afford this seemingly never-ending battery of tests.

To add further insult to this humiliating process, I had a great deal of difficulty finding a preceptor to work with me. Despite the professional connections I'd made over the decades, most of the physicians I contacted said they weren't able to act as a preceptor. While I'm sure that many of them did have legitimate reasons not to help, I couldn't help but wonder how many of them turned me down because of the charges that had been brought against me. How many of them believed that those charges were true? I still wasn't certain that my wife and children had ever come to trust me, so why should I believe that other doctors would give me the benefit of the doubt when my family had not? And how many of the doctors who believed that I'd been guilty of prescription fraud also believed that I should never be allowed to practice medicine again because of it? Honestly, how eager would I myself have been to help a doctor convicted of such a crime to get his medical license back?

After writing literally a hundred letters to a hundred different doctors and getting rejected by all of them, I was finally able to find a doctor who would act as my preceptor. After that, I needed to return to Denver to complete another set of tests, this time with the focus on my understanding of internal medicine (my other specialty). This set of tests cost me three thousand dollars plus air fare and hotel accommodations. Once again, I was able to pass these tests without any difficulty, save the financial burden they placed on me.

What followed was eleven months of gradually increasing responsibility as I slowly proved to both the preceptor and CPEP that I was in fact still qualified to practice medicine. During this period, I reported to the Denver office once a month (with an accompanying charge of two hundred dollars per visit, as well as travel and lodging expenses). My preceptor consistently told them that I was doing well; again, I don't know why this entire process needed to take longer than a year.

At the end of fourteen months (three months of study and eleven months with the preceptor), it was time for me to finish my post-education testing. Again, this required a trip to Denver, as well as three thousand dollars to take the test. I was able to complete the test without any trouble. I'm sure that I could have passed it without the fourteen months of pointless testing and exorbitant fees.

Although I finished my test in December of 2016, I was told that the grading would take three or four months, during which time I would need to simply wait. For three thousand dollars, I guess I should have expected an in-depth grading process, but I still couldn't understand what took people so long to grade a test.

Between the expenses of the tests themselves, as well as travel and accommodations, I had easily spent over ten thousand dollars on this stage of getting my license back. I can't imagine how people who were bad at poker could afford to get their licenses reinstated.

Chapter Twenty-Six

mentioned that I had some difficulty in finding a preceptor. At first, I sent out a hundred letters to a hundred different pulmonary specialists throughout Kentucky. This ended with my receiving one hundred rejection letters. I then switched to searching for a preceptor with a background in internal medicine. Throughout this process, I was hoping to find someone who was unfamiliar with my background and who wouldn't judge me based on my criminal conviction. But it turned out that the doctor who finally agreed to work with me was someone I'd known for years. I'd first met William Godfrey when I had begun my private practice more than twenty years earlier. Like me, he'd specialized in internal medicine. Since I was also a pulmonologist, Dr. Godfrey would frequently refer his patients to me when they were having lung troubles.

Another thing that Dr. Godfrey and I had in common was that we had both invested in several properties. But while most of my property investments were either residential buildings or office suites, he had chosen to invest in a fitness center. The E-Town Swim and Fitness Center was established both with his own money and the money he got from selling shares to many of his fellow doctors. Teresa and I had even bought a few shares of the center, believing it was a sound investment. And over the years, we were proven right. In addition to being an early investor, I was also a member of the fitness center and used it frequently.

Besides the fact that I'd known him for years, William and I both had a background in internal medicine, meaning that when I observed his work, I would be observing a practice similar to the one I would be returning to. Best of all, he didn't seem at all bothered by the fact that I had been convicted on prescription fraud charges. Whether he believed that I was innocent or that I had sufficiently paid for my crimes…I never bothered to ask. I was just relieved to find someone who was willing to help me with this final stage in the licensing process.

William expected to get something in return for his help. Specifically, he wanted me to sell him my two shares of his fitness center. Since he'd founded the place, he'd slowly begun buying shares back from the doctors who had originally invested in the place. In most of those cases, I'm sure that he offered them a fair price for shares in what had become a very successful enterprise. However, in my case, the price he offered was five thousand dollars, and, while the shares were worth at least twice that much, I had little choice but to agree. He was the only doctor I knew who not only shared one of my specialties but was also willing to work as a preceptor for a convicted criminal.

Since the shares belonged to my wife as well as to me, Teresa needed to sign off on this deal as well. Needless to say, she was upset. She was painfully aware that every stage of getting my medical license back came with a price tag (often thousands of dollars). Over the last decade, all my former patients had gone on to find other physicians, so I would need to find new patients when I was finally able to start my practice again. On top of that, I was already in my late sixties, and there was a question of how many more years I would be able to practice medicine once I managed to get my license back. I could tell that Teresa had begun calculating how much money I stood to earn as a doctor over my remaining lifetime against how much money it would cost for me to be able to practice medicine again.

But my efforts to regain my medical license were about more than simply having another source of income at my disposal. I'd originally entered the medical profession because being a doctor meant being respected. When I lost my license, I felt that I also lost the trust and respect of my patients, my fellow physicians, and even my family. Even if I never made back the money I had to spend to get my license reinstated, I wanted to get back that part of my life. It was a part of my life that I'd more than earned.

After the three months spent studying medicine, I was able to begin working directly with Dr. Godfrey. For our first three months together, I was merely required to observe Dr. Godfrey while he met with patients. This was the sort of thing that I'd done when I was first studying medicine back in the early 1970s. I'd done more than simply observe even back during my residency training at the University of Louisville. But CPEP required that I spend three months watching how a doctor worked, as if I didn't know as much about practicing medicine as my preceptor.

To make matters even worse, once I began sitting in on his patient visits, Dr. Godfrey changed the deal we'd made. Where he'd originally said that he would only work as my preceptor if I sold him my shares for half their value, he now said that he wouldn't work with me unless I gave him the shares outright—for free! At the time, they were worth about $11,000. Because of the way he'd timed this new demand, I either had to give him the shares or abandon the process I'd already invested half a year into. So he got his free shares.

After three months of observing Dr. Godfrey, I could finally begin seeing patients again. At that point, Dr. Godfrey still needed to be present whenever I was with a patient. I was working out of his practice rather than out of the building that I'd built more than twenty years ago for my own practice. And the patients I saw weren't actually my own patients, but Dr. Godfrey's. It was similar to what our arrangement had been more than a decade earlier, when he would refer patients to me when they had lung conditions that were outside of his experience. The key difference was that I was no longer being treated like an equal, but more like a student. I'm sure that many of these patients thought that I was seeing them in order to amass a certain number of hours of hands-on experience, as if I were a student and Dr. Godfrey was doing me a favor. How many of them would have believed that, fifteen years earlier, Dr. Godfrey would only send me patients when they had conditions he couldn't treat?

After three months of seeing patients under Dr. Godfrey's observation, I was finally allowed to see patients without him being present. I still needed to report to him every two weeks. I was in fact still working out of the same building as him. And I only worked one day a week. But I finally began to feel close to getting my medical license back. At that point, I imagined that I just needed to get my test results back and then I could finally start my practice again.

Unfortunately, a few more complications still awaited me.

Chapter Twenty-Seven

Eventually, Dr. Godfrey wrote a letter to the Kentucky Medical Board, stating that I could practice medicine on my own again. This letter was received in December of 2016, around the same time that I was finishing up my post-education testing with CPEP. So, at that point, all I needed to do was wait for the results from those final tests to come back, and then I could restart my practice again. At that point, I had no reason to believe I wouldn't pass that final test, so I began planning for my future.

At the start of 2017, I was no longer working even one day a week at Dr. Godfrey's practice, so my "retraining" was complete, but I was not yet able to practice medicine on my own again. I sat at home, waiting for CPEP to send my test results.

When I'm sitting at home with nothing to do is when I begin to make my biggest plans. I was sitting at home with nothing to do when I decided to become a chef. I was sitting at home with nothing to do when I decided to become a professional poker player. And now I was sitting at home with nothing to do again, thinking about what I would do with my life once I finally got back my medical license.

Over the past decade and a half, I'd come to depend on my various property investments, as well as the occasional poker tournament, for money. My wife had a successful medical practice of her own. And since all our children were grown up, we didn't have as many bills to worry about. So I didn't really need to practice medicine for money any longer.

While staying in Vietnam, I'd started an intensive care unit. Not only had I been involved in the basic setup and day-to-day administration of that ICU, but I'd also introduced a different type of medical treatment to the area, a method that involved treating patients with more respect than they were accustomed to receiving, even when they weren't able to pay for medical treatment up front. Despite the objections I'd received from other doctors, the ICU had been successful.

So why not start a clinic here in the United States? I already had a building that I could use; I could treat patients myself, as well as oversee other doctors. There was legal paperwork to go through, but I already had a lawyer I trusted with a background in medical law. There would be up-front expenses involved in starting a clinic, but I had the money.

That left one big question: who would be treated in my clinic? If I wasn't worried about making a lot of money, who would I want to treat?

As I sat at home, thinking about this clinic I wanted to build, I remembered the journey I'd originally made to this country. More than forty years ago, I had been on a boat in the Pacific Ocean, not sure where I would end up or even how long I would be able to survive. Only much later did I learn how many people had died making that same journey. I remembered how grateful I'd been to see an American Navy ship and how well the crewmembers had treated us. Forty years later, I wondered how many of those crewmembers were struggling. There were too many veterans in this country who weren't able to afford basic necessities like shelter, much less medical treatment. Many of them were also suffering from PTSD, just as I was, after dealing with the same war that had driven me from my home country. I had been helped by these people so many years ago, back when I had nothing to offer in return but my gratitude. But now I could offer them so much more.

So, during the early months of 2017, I began making plans to open a veterans' clinic. While I couldn't yet treat patients, I could certainly begin the preliminary work for setting up a clinic. At first, I would treat the patients by myself, but in time, I might be able to hire on more doctors to help me. As for finding the patients, I knew that plenty of veterans throughout this country were unable to afford quality medical care. I began placing ads in the local newspapers to reach out to them; while this might not be the most efficient method of reaching younger veterans, who tend to get most of their information from the Internet, it is quite effective for reaching older men and women who still rely on the daily newspaper for information about their community.

It's worth mentioning that, if I hadn't already set up an intensive care unit in Vietnam, I might have doubted whether or not I'd be able to set up a veterans' clinic in Elizabethtown. And I wouldn't have set up that ICU if I hadn't been able to spend ten months in Vietnam. And I wouldn't have been able to spend ten months in Vietnam if my license hadn't been suspended. If my license hadn't been suspended, I might never have even considered setting up a clinic to help veterans.

Had everything I'd gone through over these last sixteen years been a part of God's plan for me? Had the false accusation, my conviction, and the loss of my medical practice all been designed to drive me to a higher purpose? People ask how God can be good if he allows bad things to happen. Sometimes, those bad things are necessary in order to make great work possible. Soon, I was given another lesson demonstrating this verity to me.

Chapter Twenty-Eight

By April of 2017, I was sixty-nine years old and still trying to get my medical license fully reinstated. I desperately wanted to continue practicing medicine, while many doctors my age had either retired or were seriously considering retirement. During this time, Teresa and I received invitations to the Saigon University's fifty-year class reunion. I hadn't graduated from medical school until after 1967. And Teresa had graduated a year after I did. However, due to small class sizes and the fact that organizing an annual reunion could be difficult, it was decided that everyone who'd graduated between 1967 and 1974 would be included in a single reunion.

I was conflicted about attending my class reunion at this point. Not only was I still not working, but I didn't want to recount the last fifteen years of my life to every one of my former classmates. I already had to deal with judgment from so many physicians in Kentucky. I didn't want any other doctors passing judgment on me based on nothing more than the assumption that innocent men don't get convicted.

On the other hand, I had accomplished quite a lot during my forty-two years in the United States. I was married and had five children. I had participated in many well-known marathons. I had enjoyed some success as a tournament poker player. I had returned to

Vietnam to establish an intensive care unit. I had become a chef. I had continued playing in my band and had organized a charity concert.

And if all those accomplishments weren't good enough reasons to attend, then there was the fact that my wife was herself a successful doctor and she shouldn't have to miss the reunion because of the troubles I was going through. As it was, Teresa had put up with too much because of my legal troubles already.

The final deciding factor was the fact that this was our fifty-year class reunion and there would never be another one. So, if we didn't attend this time, we likely would never see many of our old classmates again.

So, on April 6, Teresa and I arrived in Los Angeles. We met with nearly a hundred other graduates as well as three of our instructors in Westminster. Since I didn't know many of these graduates all too well (because they'd been students either before or after me), it was easy to keep the conversations vague enough that I never had to mention losing my medical license. Teresa and I both had a great time, and I even performed a song I wrote specifically for the reunion during the banquet.

Many of the graduates in attendance lived in California. It made sense, since most of us came to the United States as refugees after the war, and California would naturally be where most of the ships docked. Teresa and I had both spent some time in California upon our respective arrivals before we each moved to other states.

At one point, several of the graduates had the idea of taking a cruise down to Mexico together. While this was easy enough to plan for the ones who lived in California, those of us from out of state would need to make special plans and rebook our flights if we wanted to go along. Still, Teresa and I were having a nice enough time at the reunion that we placed ourselves on a waiting list for the cruise. But, as it turned out, no spots opened up for us, so we took our scheduled flight back to Kentucky.

You probably know what happened next.

Chapter Twenty-Nine

Originally, our flight was scheduled to go from Los Angeles to Louisville, with a stop in Denver. But when we arrived at the airport, we were told that the flight had been switched so that the stop would now be in Chicago. We were on board the Chicago to Louisville flight by five o'clock Sunday night.

I was eager to return to Kentucky. After catching up with fellow physicians over the weekend, I knew that many of my classmates were already making plans for their retirement. I, on the other hand, was getting ready to start a whole new chapter in my medical career. After years of being unable to practice medicine, I was not only ready to practice on my own again, but to open a whole new clinic. I was still waiting for CPEP to finish evaluating my test, but there were plenty of other things I needed to do in the meantime to set up a clinic.

And Teresa still had a thriving pediatric practice of her own, and she didn't want to miss work either. She had patients depending on her and, as anyone who has children knows, an appointment with a pediatrician involves both a parent taking time off from a job and picking up a child from school. Since parents bringing in their children often have to juggle two schedules (their own and their child's), planning such appointments can be difficult. And none of her patients would appreciate being told that those appointments would have to be rescheduled at the last minute.

At about twenty minutes after five o'clock, an employee with United Airlines came on board and told us that four United Airlines employees needed to board our flight. Since the flight was already overbooked, that meant that four of the passengers currently seated needed to volunteer to leave. Neither Teresa nor I were willing to leave the plane. We'd already settled into our seats. Our seatbelts were fastened in preparation for takeoff. Looking around, I saw that nobody else was volunteering to deboard the plane either.

We were then told that anyone who volunteered to get off the plane would be given a four-hundred-dollar voucher that could be used on a future United Airlines flight. They would also be placed on another flight to Louisville, but that flight wouldn't be leaving for at least another twenty-one hours (assuming that there were no delays or other employees who needed to reach Louisville at the last minute). In addition, the airline would pay for the passengers to stay in a hotel overnight. Still, nobody volunteered.

The representative then left the flight for a short time and returned to let us know that the voucher they were offering had now been raised to eight hundred dollars. When even then nobody volunteered to get off the plane, a manager came on board and told us that four passengers were going to be chosen by computer. The way that she made it sound, I guess we were supposed to believe that the process was random.

My wife and I, as well as another couple, were told that we'd been selected by computer to leave the flight. Teresa and I remained buckled in our seats while the other couple complied without any objection. While we couldn't believe what was happening, I could also see things from the other couple's point of view. After all, a computer had selected us; it had been a random process, and there was nothing we could do about it.

But there had been too many times in my life when things had happened and I'd been told that there was nothing that anyone could do about it. The years I'd spent in the United States, recertifying to get a medical license that I'd already earned in Vietnam. The two and a half years I hadn't been able to practice medicine while waiting for a trial to occur. The guilty verdict that had destroyed my reputation and my practice, despite there being no evidence against me. The years that I'd spent taking test after test, spending tens of thousands of dollars in the process, all because that was the system and nobody could beat the system, even when it made no sense.

And then I thought about the times when I'd said no: I remembered the backward way music had been taught at the conservatory. I remembered nearly losing my place in a residency program due to an alleged language barrier. I remembered seeing the way that medicine was still being practiced in Vietnam. In every one of those situations, I'd been told that there was nothing I could do, that there was no decision for me to make.

But when I'd led the protest at the conservatory, the minister of culture and the director of the music program had both admitted that there was no reason that music had to be taught in such an arbitrary and unstructured manner. When I'd pressed the program director at the University of Louisville, he'd turned over my evaluation report and admitted that there were no complaints about a language barrier (or my job performance in general). When I'd established the intensive care unit, many of the doctors who'd initially objected to my method of practicing medicine eventually adopted that method for themselves. All it had taken to change things was one person asking why things were done that way and suggesting a different way.

So, when a woman identifying herself as a supervisor asked me to leave my seat, I said, "No." I explained that my wife and I were both doctors and that we had patients waiting to see us in Louisville the following day. Perhaps two other passengers could be chosen. Or perhaps the United Airlines employees could take the later flight, since we'd paid for our tickets and had already been seated.

At this point, the supervisor told me that if I didn't leave my seat, she would call the police. I'd had bad experiences dealing with police officers in the past. I knew that sometimes the police didn't care about getting all the facts straight so much as they cared about settling problems. And that was all that Teresa and I were going to be if the police arrived: a problem to be solved as quickly as possible. If the quickest solution was pulling me off a plane, then that's what they would do. And if they needed justification, they'd simply say that the computer had chosen us.

But then I thought about my residency at the University of Louisville. The director had insisted that there had been complaints about my accent and my grasp of the English language. He'd said it with such authority, and he'd seemed to be genuinely shocked when I had asked to see the report. He'd no doubt expected that I would simply take his word for it. After all, there was absolutely no reason why he would have lied about such a thing. Except that the report had included nothing about my accent or grasp of English. The report had included no complaints about me at all.

Everyone else was willing to accept that a computer chose passenger names at random to yield their seats on planes in cases of overbooking. But none of us had seen this process occur. What if there was no such computer? What if our names had been chosen in some other way, perhaps based on how much trouble the airline believed we would cause? Or maybe it was based on something even simpler and uglier?

Had I been chosen because my last name was "Dao?" Was it just simple racism? I remember asking the supervisor if Teresa and I had been chosen because we were Asian. She had no answer.

I saw three security guards approaching me. I would later find out that these were officers from the Chicago Department of Aviation, not members of the Chicago Police Department. While I didn't know it at the time, they did not have the power to arrest me. But they did physically take hold of me and pull me out of my seat.

At this point, I began screaming. Even if there had been a computer that randomly selected passengers to be removed from a plane, what these security guards were doing couldn't possibly be legal. Looking around, I saw that none of the passengers were getting up to help me. I honestly don't know if the situation would have been better or worse if the other passengers had intervened; in fact, there's a good chance that things could have escalated into something much worse if they had. Thankfully, I learned later that several of them had their smartphones out.

I continued screaming as the security guards tried to drag me out of the plane. At one point, I was thrown toward one of the seats. I remember hearing a loud noise.

And that was it. I don't remember anything else that happened.

Chapter Thirty

My next memory was waking up in pain. I was in an emergency room, and a doctor was stitching up a suture in my mouth. I found out that I had been brought to a trauma unit because of my injuries. In addition to the suture in my lip, I also needed to have a suture in my nose. I'd lost two of my teeth as well. I couldn't remember much about what had happened on the plane, and I should have immediately begun asking questions, but on top of everything else, I was suffering from a terrible headache that made thinking clearly difficult.

Nobody in the emergency room offered any information about what had happened to me, and I couldn't focus enough to think to ask. Instead, I went along with the various tests they put me through to determine the extent of my injuries. At one point, they even administered a CT scan to get a better idea of the head injuries I'd suffered.

After four hours of tests, I was diagnosed with a concussion and placed in a room. Teresa was there, waiting for me. By this point, it was so late and I was so exhausted from the tests that I simply fell asleep.

When I woke up the next morning, Teresa was still there. I was feeling disoriented from my head injury, as well as from whatever painkillers I'd been given. At the time, I didn't think to ask her anything.

Our daughter Crystal had moved to Chicago a couple of years earlier, so she was able to visit my room shortly after I woke up. She brought her husband Jake with her. I could only assume that Teresa had called all our children while I'd been in the trauma unit, because Crystal and Jake already knew what had happened. In my disoriented state, I wasn't sure how my daughter would react. After all, she might have assumed that I'd done something wrong and that the security guards had been right in using excessive force to remove me from the plane. She might also have assumed that my injuries were the result of an accident and that I shouldn't blame the security guards for what had happened. Some of my concerns were colored by my previous experience of being accused of prescription fraud, when nobody believed in my innocence. But this time, Crystal made it clear that she wholeheartedly believed me and that she agreed that I had done nothing wrong.

Crystal even told me that she'd contacted her attorney and that we would be bringing a suit against United Airlines. At this point, I hadn't even considered a lawsuit, not because the security guards were innocent, but because I couldn't imagine being able to prove what they'd done. A court case would be my word against theirs, and I knew from past experience that innocent people didn't always win court cases. My wife and some of the passengers had seen the attack as well, but I didn't know if that would be enough.

Still, I was glad that my daughter believed me, and I hoped that my other children would believe me as well. I didn't know anything about the media coverage, so I thought they only knew about the incident based on what Teresa and I had told them.

Crystal and Jake eventually left the hospital, assuring me that they'd be back later in the day with an attorney. Before leaving, Crystal took my telephone away from me. She also told me not to watch any television. At the time, I was too groggy to question why she'd done either of those things.

Chapter Thirty-One

Throughout the day, I was visited by various doctors. An ENT (ear, nose, and throat) specialist checked on the damage to my nose. My eyes were checked out by an ophthalmologist. A neurologist came in to speak with me about the CT scan results. I've heard that doctors make the worst patients, but I was still disoriented, so I didn't argue with any of them.

I knew that after I got some sleep, I would soon become desperate to get out of bed, but during that first day in the hospital, I mostly wanted to rest between answering the doctors' questions. I would have liked to call my other children and let them know that I was doing all right, but I assumed that Teresa was keeping everyone up to date. Besides, I couldn't call anyone since my daughter had taken my phone.

But why would she do that? I got the impression that if Crystal could have had the television removed from my room, she would have done so as well. As it was, she had taken my phone, so I wasn't able to call anyone…or check the Internet. There was no radio in the room either.

That's when I began to wonder if Crystal was trying to keep something from me. Perhaps one of my children had been injured. Or maybe there was some new development in my ongoing effort to get my medical license fully reinstated. Teresa would have known about anything like that…but maybe she had thought it was better to keep bad news from me while I was in the hospital. I was still too groggy to tell if she was deliberately hiding something from me, but it did seem odd that she hadn't questioned our daughter about taking my phone away. What did she think I was going to do with a phone…besides call someone or check my email?

If Teresa and Crystal just wanted to hide a family issue from me, taking away my telephone would have been enough. But Crystal had also told me not to watch television. That meant that whatever she didn't want me to know was something that would be on the news. If it was a local emergency situation (like a tornado), then the hospital staff would have likely said something. So it was probably some sort of tragedy. Maybe a tornado or hurricane had struck some other part of the world. Perhaps an earthquake. Or it might have been an accident like a high-rise fire. Maybe a plane crash. Or maybe there had been a terrorist attack.

I became convinced that there was something on the news that Crystal and Teresa didn't want me to see. While they'd both told me to get some sleep, I knew that wouldn't be possible until I knew what was wrong. I turned on the television and began flipping through the channels in search of the great disaster that I wasn't supposed to see.

At first, I didn't find anything horrible that had happened: no natural disasters or accidents or terrorist attacks. It had just been another day.

And then I saw a video of a bloodied man, screaming as he was being dragged off a plane.

A number of the other passengers had uploaded their phone videos to social media sites. Those videos had been shared and reposted thousands of times over the next few hours.

The media had found several of the other passengers and gathered more information about what had happened to me after I'd initially lost consciousness. I learned that, after I'd been taken off the plane, many of the other passengers had deboarded as well. At the point when I finally saw the news about the incident, United Airlines had not yet issued a formal statement on the incident.

The newscasters reported that I was in stable condition but had not yet made any statement.

I remember crying as I went from channel to channel, trying to find out more about what had happened. Teresa sat beside me, watching as I took it all in. She said nothing, and, at first, I couldn't think of anything to say to her. I know that Crystal hadn't wanted me to watch the news because she thought seeing a video of myself bloody and screaming would upset me. But I wasn't crying because of the way I'd been treated on the plane. I was crying because the people who'd sat around me on that plane, the ones I thought had done nothing while I was being dragged away, had been recording the incident. They'd posted those videos after walking off the plane. The news media had picked up the story and run with it. Over and over again, I heard them comment about how shocking and disgusting my treatment had been.

That's why Crystal had taken away my phone and asked me not to watch any television. She was worried that I might catch some of the local stations' coverage of the event.

Chapter Thirty-Two

By the time Crystal and Jake returned that afternoon, I was well aware that the news media was covering the incident. As promised, they had their lawyer, Stephen Golan, with them. But it turned out that Stephen's specialties were estate management and corporate law, so he wasn't the best person to represent me in this particular case. However, he managed to secure another attorney, Thomas Demetrio, who had an extensive background in aviation law. In fact, it was something of a coincidence that the best possible lawyer I could have hired to represent me happened to work in Chicago.

I could honestly fill an entire book listing Tom's accomplishments as a lawyer. He has repeatedly been cited as one of the best trial lawyers in the country. He had served as president of the Chicago Bar Association. His previous work in aviation law included trials and settlements in a number of plane and helicopter crashes, including the crashes that took the lives of Jim Croce and Stevie Ray Vaughan. He'd also represented players (and their families) in suits against both the NHL and the NFL involving concussion injuries. Not only was I glad to have someone with his experience representing me, but I admired the man for the work he did.

The handful of reports on television hadn't told me everything I needed to know. I asked Crystal to give me back my phone so I could go online and get a better idea of what people were saying. However, she refused to give my phone back—and wouldn't return it to me until I was back home in Kentucky.

I was still feeling groggy from my head injury, simply trying to grasp what had happened. What I had initially thought would be a personal stand that I'd taken against United Airlines had now become something much bigger. Not only did I have doctors who would testify regarding my physical injuries, but I also had video footage of the attack to back me up. On top of that, I had one of the best lawyers in the country representing me. It was a lot to take in, and I wanted to spend a few days considering my options, gathering my thoughts, and talking with my family about what I should do.

Obviously, United Airlines wanted this whole event to be resolved and then hopefully forgotten by the general public within the next few days. And while none of us had spoken directly with United at that stage, Tom was confident that they would be willing to make a significant offer.

I knew there was another reason why Tom wanted to settle with United Airlines sooner rather than later. At that point, all that was being said about me was that I had been injured while being dragged off an airplane. But the longer we waited to settle, the more likely it was that some reporter would uncover my arrest and conviction from years earlier. While that case had nothing to do with what had happened on the plane, my conviction was not something I wanted to relive. I was planning to open a clinic soon, and those charges were better as forgotten fifteen-year-old news.

For the next four days, I remained in the hospital. I saw a variety of specialists, including a psychologist. Physically, I was recovering at a steady pace, although I was still suffering from terrible headaches. Mentally, I continued to have difficulty focusing on anything for long, and I didn't want to decide on the case until I had fully recovered, both physically and mentally.

By the time I was ready to leave the hospital, the media had uncovered the story of my arrest. Fortunately, I didn't have my phone, so nobody was able to reach me. I was sure that Tom's law firm was fielding some calls about my case, but at the time, I hadn't realized how big this story had become, so it had never occurred to me that my wife or children might have been receiving calls as well.

If you've ever been hospitalized, you probably know that the day you're allowed to leave is not the day when you're fully recovered. I was still healing physically, but other than the headaches, my physical injuries were largely cosmetic at that point: missing teeth, sutures, bruises. Mentally, gauging exactly how much damage had been done by the concussion was more difficult; a psychologist had said that I was recovered enough to leave, but I still had trouble focusing and difficulty sleeping. I would have liked to have gone home to spend a few days resting in my own bed. Unfortunately, that wasn't an option.

While I was in the hospital, the staff did an excellent job of keeping news reporters away from me, but I'd been told that, once I left, they would be waiting for me. Ordinarily, I would have welcomed the chance to speak with a reporter about what had happened on the plane. I would have even been willing to discuss my arrest from years earlier. But while I was recovering from a head injury, there was a good chance that I would make some sort of misstatement or misstep. I might have described the event and given the wrong number of security guards or mistaken someone's name or gotten the flight number wrong. When talking about my arrest in 2003, I might have said something about the arresting officer, one of the police detectives, BC, or one of my lawyers that could be misinterpreted as slander. Or I might have been short-tempered due to a headache. Any of these understandable reactions would then be broadcast and used as proof that I was unreliable, a liar, or even violent.

Tom had told me not to speak with the media. Since so much of the damage that United was trying to minimize had to do with public perception, anything I said could have an effect on that perception, one way or the other, and thus influence the negotiation. Avoiding the media was easier said than done. And I didn't want to get on another plane anytime soon.

When I left the hospital, I ended up staying with Crystal and Jake at their house for four days.

My medical license was still restricted, despite my having finished my tests with CPEC four months earlier. I hadn't been able to do any work on setting up a clinic since leaving Kentucky two weeks earlier for the class reunion. Even if I was back home, I couldn't imagine being able to do anything productive in my current condition.

Crystal and Jake did what they could to make me feel comfortable, but I could tell that something was bothering them. At the time, I still didn't know how big this story had become, so I imagined that the news media was only trying to get in touch with me. I didn't know that my daughter was also being approached by reporters. In fact, I didn't know much of anything that was happening in the world outside of their house because she still wouldn't give me back my phone. On top of that, I was discouraged from even going outside. In a lot of ways, I felt as if I was under house arrest or part of some witness relocation program. Eventually, I felt like I was in prison. I couldn't have any contact with the outside world, and no one would tell me how long this situation would last.

Between the lingering effects of my concussion and the depression I was feeling over being confined, my condition began to deteriorate, and I was readmitted to the hospital. Now, I wasn't even able to sleep in a normal bed in relative quiet. I was back to a noisy hospital with no privacy and even less contact with my family. At one point, I closed my eyes and wished that everything would just stop.

Unfortunately, when I made that wish, I spoke it out loud. One of the nurses heard me wishing that I could shut my eyes and never wake up again and came to what must have seemed like an obvious conclusion. I spent the next four days in the hospital under a suicide watch. That meant that whatever limited privacy I might have enjoyed in the hospital was gone, as a nurse would be present in my room twenty-four hours a day, literally watching me to make sure I didn't kill myself.

I just wanted to go home.

When I was finally released from the hospital once again, Crystal thought it might be better if she found a place where Teresa and I could stay on our own. She had a friend who was out of town for a few weeks who said we could stay at her house for a while. This setup provided me with a sense of privacy (which was especially welcome after the exposure of being on a suicide watch), and it made it more difficult for reporters to find me. More than two weeks had now passed since the incident on the airplane, and I couldn't understand why anyone was still worried about it. I certainly wasn't seeing it covered in the local news any longer, and I doubted that the few people who had heard about the incident even remembered it any longer.

Tom called me to discuss my case, including an offer of settlement from United Airlines. I still wanted to wait until I'd fully recovered. I wanted to wait until I was at least able to spend a few nights sleeping in my own bed again. I wanted to wait until my daughter returned my telephone so I could do some research and get a better perspective on the situation. I always did a lot of studying before I made a decision, whether it was to become a doctor, a musician, a professional poker player, an investor, an ICU director, or a chef.

I had nearly finished going through a sixteen-year ordeal to get my medical license back. That process had involved numerous different tests. It had involved interviews with therapists, doctors, and board members, as well as a seemingly endless amount of paperwork. It had involved a few difficult deals. Frankly, after everything I'd gone through with CPEP, the Kentucky Medical Board, and Pine Grove, I figured that I could handle questions from a few reporters. Throughout my life, my problems only seemed to get worse when I stepped back and let other people handle things their way.

I was sick of being a prisoner in the hospital, in my daughter's home, and now in a stranger's house. I went for a walk. It was something I had often done when I wanted to relax or just clear my head. I simply put on my shoes and walked out the front door, as if I was an innocent man with nothing to hide…which is all that I'd ever been.

Jake showed up within minutes. I don't know how he found out I'd left the house, but he pulled up right beside me in his car and asked me to get in. I don't know what he thought was going to happen to me. There were no hordes of reporters waiting to ask me questions. Nobody was taking my picture. Nobody even noticed a sixty-nine-year-old man taking a walk through the neighborhood, but Jake was insistent that I get in his car immediately.

I then had to explain to my son-in-law why I didn't want to be trapped in a house any longer, as if it was the sort of thing that I had to explain—as if anyone would want to spend their days inside a stranger's house, never going out, never allowed to make phone calls or even check the Internet.

So, my family finally allowed me to return to Kentucky. In order to avoid being noticed, it was decided that my son Ben (who had come in from Syracuse, New York, to visit me) would drive me back, as opposed to my getting on board another airplane. The drive took several hours, but after almost three weeks, I was back in my home. On top of that, when I got home, I also got my phone back. The first thing I did was check my messages. Then I went online for the first time in weeks.

And then I understood all of it: why I'd been kept in hiding and why all my children had seemed so uncomfortable about what had happened. I had thought this incident was just a local story in Chicago. I'd thought that I could get away from the media simply by leaving the city.

But this story had been reported around the world. I'd unwittingly become a celebrity.

Chapter Thirty-Three

Over the years, I had experienced some minor celebrity from time to time. My music band, Bach Viet, had made a few television appearances back in Vietnam. The benefit concert I'd organized years earlier in Seattle had received quite a bit of media coverage. I'd participated in several well-known marathons. My arrest and trial fifteen years earlier had garnered quite a bit of attention as well, albeit wholly unwanted attention. Even professional poker playing had earned me a sort of celebrity status.

All of which is to say that I wasn't afraid of getting some more attention because of what had happened on the United Airlines flight. In fact, I wanted to speak with the media about what had happened. After a month of hiding, I wanted to talk about it. But before I could say anything, I was overwhelmed by what everyone else was saying about me. And by "everyone else," I mean people from all over the world.

You probably first heard about my story through social media. Maybe you saw a link to a news article or maybe a link to that video. Or maybe you first found out about it when one of your friends offered an opinion. Lots of people had opinions about the incident. I spent days reading them—so many opinions. If people from around the world were talking about something that happened to you, wouldn't you spend days reading it all?

The overwhelming majority of people posting on the incident agreed that what had happened to me was wrong. While that might seem obvious, I was not accustomed to people giving me the benefit of the doubt. For all I knew, the general public could have chosen to side with United Airlines on this matter. At first, it seemed as if the upper management of the airline company was going to dig in its heels and defend the decision to forcibly remove me from an airplane that I'd paid to be on. But once more facts in the case came out, United Airlines acknowledged that a mistake had been made.

But while thousands of people I'd never met and even United Airlines itself agreed that what had happened to me was wrong, others chose to argue that my treatment had been justified. I don't know if those people were motivated by a belief that bad things couldn't possibly happen to innocent people or by simple racism. Some people just have an instinctive desire to play "devil's advocate" in any situation. Whatever the reason, I saw a few defenses being brought forward for what had happened.

One defense was that it was written right on my ticket that United Airlines had the right to deny me a seat I'd paid for on an airplane. I checked, and this is absolutely true. But is anyone really expected to read the fine print on those tickets? Do you read through the user agreement on every piece of software you download on your computer? Did you read through the copyright page of this book? When we got on the plane, a set of instructions for what to do in case of an emergency had been placed on the seat in front us; yet the airline had considered it necessary for a flight attendant to walk us through the safety procedures anyway. So why would they assume that we'd read the fine print on our tickets? Did you know that an airline can legally throw you off a flight for no reason other than that they decide to give someone else your seat?

Another defense was that I'd somehow deserved what had happened to me. Some people wondered if I'd been aggressive on the airplane and somehow provoked the response from the security personnel. Within the first few days of the incident, my previous arrest and conviction had been linked to the story, so that somehow what had happened to me fifteen years earlier was supposed to justify what had happened on the plane. Not surprisingly, a variety of different sources were used for that story, and there were plenty of conflicting accounts. Since I wasn't speaking with anyone at that point besides my family and my attorneys, nobody was able to get the story correct.

The ironic part about bringing up my previous conviction is that it seemed to turn public opinion even further against United Airlines. Many people agreed that what had happened to me in 2003 had no relevance to what was happening in 2017. And when people think you're trying to divert their attention, that usually only sharpens their focus. So, while it was embarrassing to have my arrest and conviction brought onto a global stage, in the end it only helped to win more sympathy for my case.

I even saw some stories concerning a Dr. David Dao who was working in Louisiana. I suppose I could see the confusion of one Dr. David Dao living in Louisiana while another had previously lived in Louisville. And I imagine that it was even more frustrating that the Dr. Dao who was answering his calls after the incident was in fact not the one that the news reporters were trying to reach.

One thing I noticed was that opinions about this incident were especially strong in Vietnam and other Asian countries. While American readers were quick to focus on the excessive nature of the security guards' response, most of them didn't seem to believe that I'd been specifically targeted for this treatment, as if this sort of occurrence was just as likely to have happened to anyone else on the plane. Asian readers, on the other hand, were concerned about whether I was being targeted because of my ethnicity. This incident occurred only a couple of months after a series of travel bans were issued that focused on Middle Eastern countries. Around the world, people were talking about xenophobic attitudes in the United States, and what happened to me was being interpreted by many as evidence of a prejudice against Asian people.

Through it all, people wondered when I would make a statement. My attorney had made it clear to me why I shouldn't make any public statements until an agreement was reached with United Airlines. It was now far clearer to me why the airline was eager to put this whole matter behind them. While I understood why a cash settlement created a clear incentive for them to avoid such incidents in the future, I also wanted to make sure that steps were taken so that what had happened to me wouldn't happen to anyone else.

Most of all, I wanted to take some time to review all this new information before I agreed to anything. I was still absorbing the sheer scale of the coverage. This had become a global event that even the president of the United States had seen fit to weigh in on. At one point, he was asked about the incident during an interview. Donald Trump summed up my treatment by United Airlines with a single word: "Horrible."

But there was more than just myself and United Airlines to consider. While I had been successfully shielded from the media, my wife and children hadn't been so fortunate. When the news media outlets hadn't been able to find me, they'd begun tracking down my family. My daughter Crystal was easy enough to find, since the incident had happened in Chicago and she lived there. She even appeared with Tom for a press conference several days after the incident that was viewed worldwide, and I remember crying when I finally saw the video of my daughter defending me when I was still recovering from my injuries. Once my wife had returned to her practice in Elizabethtown, her office was constantly being contacted by reporters trying to confirm that it was in fact the same practice that I had once shared with her. The fact that Teresa had been on the flight with me and witnessed the entire incident made her even more interesting to reporters.

Our son Timothy, who was working as a cardiologist in Dallas, was also regularly receiving requests for comments on the incident. Our daughter Christine, who had become a professor of medicine at the University of North Carolina, was frequently contacted by reporters. Ben, who now had an internal medicine residency in Syracuse, was being bothered. Angela was having trouble focusing on her OB/GYN residency in Cleveland because of all the media attention. News reporters would wait outside their offices, call them with a frequency verging on harassment, and even send unwanted gifts, things like bouquets of flowers, in the hope of getting some time with them. None of my children spoke with the news media, but simply carrying on with their regular lives was becoming impossible.

While I'd been frustrated about all the delays to starting my own practice again, the truth was that not having a job gave me the time I needed to recover from my injuries, as well as the solitude necessary to avoid the media. If I'd had a practice at that time, there was no way that I could have taken a month off to recover, nor would it have been possible to avoid reporters with a publicly known office address.

When I talk about my attorney recommending that I settle with the airline, the truth is that he wasn't the only one. My entire family wanted this nightmare to end. And while I would have preferred having more time to think things over as I was still suffering from headaches because of the concussion, I also understood that it wasn't fair that their lives should all be disrupted for so long. More than one of them pointed out to me that this wasn't the first time that I'd had legal problems that had spilled over into their lives. And while my arrest in 2003 hadn't been any more my fault than getting assaulted on an airplane, I knew that my family was suffering. It wasn't my fault, but it was within my power to put a stop to it.

I decided to authorize my lawyers to settle with United Airlines.

Chapter Thirty-Four

My lawyer had advised me at the time that I was within my rights to file a lawsuit against United Airlines. But for several reasons, this would have been a bad idea. First and foremost was the question of how my family was being affected by this situation. As long as the question of what I was going to do was not yet settled, a potential news story remained, and as long as a potential news story remained, my wife and children would continue to be harassed by the media, no matter where they lived.

On top of the concern for my family was also the question of how long a lawsuit would take. United Airlines wouldn't want to lose a lawsuit, so they would bring forward every argument they could muster. I knew from firsthand experience how long a seemingly straightforward case could run; it could last for months or even years.

Unfortunately, I also knew firsthand that simply because it seemed like an open-and-shut case to me wouldn't mean it would appear the same way to a judge and jury. If we filed a lawsuit against United Airlines, my attorney and I were both confident that we would eventually win it. But confidence was not a guarantee, and over the course of the trial, anything that might sway a jury's opinion could be brought up as evidence.

One of the things that might be brought into evidence would be my previous conviction. My past conviction had already been mentioned in the media coverage in an attempt to smear my reputation. I had no reason to believe that it wouldn't all be brought up again if I took United Airlines to court. Even though the earlier conviction had absolutely no relevance to what had happened on that plane, it could be brought into evidence in any number of ways, and I had no way of knowing how a jury would be affected by it. When the conviction had initially been mentioned, the effect had been to move public opinion in my favor, but there was no way of being sure that would be the case again.

There was even a chance that, as with that previous case, my attorney might decide that the best course of action would be to prevent me from taking the stand and speaking in my own defense. The result would be yet another case where I was forced to say nothing while a jury judged me by my silence. I couldn't stand doing that again.

So I chose to settle.

The settlement process concluded at the end of April. Despite everyone involved wanting this matter to be completed quickly, it still ended up taking a week to finalize the settlement. Part of the reason for that was the fact that I was not speaking directly with anyone from United Airlines. I'd learned from past experience that it was better to work through an attorney, so I would speak with Thomas, who would then contact United and get back to me with their response. While this made everything take longer, it also meant my attorney would know everything being said between us, and there wouldn't be any risk of my accidentally misstating something during the process.

These negotiations took place over the telephone; in addition to Thomas and myself, I wanted all my children and my wife to be involved in the conversations. It's truly amazing how far communication technology has come in the past few decades. My children were spread across the country, yet when I needed them, setting up a group discussion between a half-dozen people was a simple matter.

While I received a cash settlement, one of the conditions of the agreement was that I couldn't disclose the amount. Besides the money, both United Airlines and I had to agree to several other conditions. First and foremost, we each agreed not to engage in negative commenting on one another. United Airlines also began to initiate several improvements in their staff training to ensure that this sort of incident would never happen again.

By the time we were negotiating a settlement, I'd already begun thinking about how I would share my side of the story with the world. I didn't want to simply begin writing comments on different social media platforms; those formats only allow you to say so much, and it's far too easy to take a comment out of context. I wasn't against doing interviews, but even that was too limited for what I really wanted to do. My story was about more than simply getting pulled off of an airplane. My story was about becoming a doctor, fleeing Vietnam, traveling from one job to another before finally starting my own practice, meeting my wife, raising our five children, being arrested and convicted for a crime I didn't commit, accepting Jesus Christ into my life, searching for a new career, returning to Vietnam and establishing an intensive care unit, and struggling for years to regain my medical license. I also wanted to write a book that went beyond my own personal experiences to address human rights violations not only in the United States, but also in Vietnam and around the world. That couldn't be covered in any one interview. I needed to write a book, so I repeatedly reminded Thomas that, whatever agreement I eventually signed, it would have to allow me to write a book about my experience.

While nothing in the agreement required United Airlines to consult me on whatever changes they implemented, I took notice whenever they were mentioned in the news. I know that United Airlines has been more sensitive to treating their passengers with greater dignity. But more importantly, I've seen evidence that other airlines have taken steps to prevent what happened to me from happening on their flights as well. One of the specific areas that's getting a lot of attention is the practice of deliberate overbooking. I don't believe that what happened on my flight was unique to United Airlines. What they did was a result of how airlines in general treat their passengers.

In a larger sense, I feel that what happened to me was indicative of how many businesses treat their customers. We've all heard stories of people being violently removed from restaurants, clothing stores, and movie theaters. And it's not just businesses. Public services such as police departments, hospitals, and, yes, medical review boards could also make a greater effort to treat people with dignity. Too often, people are judged by their ethnicity, by their age, by their sexual orientation, or by how much money they make. When Teresa and I got on that plane, we certainly weren't wearing expensive suits, so there was no way for anyone to know that I could afford a decent lawyer or that my daughter would have the means to contact the best aviation lawyer in the country; but had we been poor with no social connections, my treatment still would have been unacceptable. I had witnessed my share of prejudicial treatment toward patients in hospitals, both in the United States and Vietnam, and I'd also learned how much difference an individual could make in such a system.

On a related note—yes, I have in fact flown on an airplane since that incident. And, yes, I've even ridden on a United Airlines flight since the incident. I didn't intentionally choose to fly on United Airlines again. I simply left my travel scheduling up to an agency, and they chose that particular airline. More than likely, the person who'd scheduled the flight had no idea who I was (so much for being a celebrity). Once I was on board, one flight attendant said, "Welcome back, Dr. Dao." After that, no mention was made of my name or the previous incident.

Once the settlement was reached, I imagined that I'd go back to living my old life. My CPEP results were due in any time, and I was looking forward to finally returning to my medical practice after so many years and false starts.

Of course, things weren't that simple.

Chapter Thirty-Five

had taken my final CPEP evaluations in December of 2016. I didn't receive the results until June of 2017. I wasn't surprised to learn that I'd passed them. I knew that I was able to practice medicine again; the tests had simply been meant to confirm it to others. Although I did wonder once again why it had taken so long for the tests to be evaluated. It hadn't taken me six months to organize a benefit concert in Seattle. It hadn't taken me six months of training before I was ready to run in my first marathon. It hadn't taken me six months to have a house built for my father and brother in Vietnam. It hadn't taken me six months to get an intensive care unit up and running. It hadn't taken me six months to go from learning the rules of poker to winning money at poker competitions. Even brokering a settlement with a major airline company regarding an internationally covered incident had only taken my lawyer a week. Why had it taken half a year to grade some papers?

Regardless of why it took so long to get the results, I was glad that the process was finally over. I'd recovered from what had happened on the airplane and come out better for the experience. I'm not referring to the cash settlement, but rather to the outpouring of support that I got from around the world. Hundreds of thousands of people from dozens of countries all expressed their outrage over what had happened to me. United Airlines had been forced to make changes in their policies because of what happened to me. My family all came together to support me. For more than ten years, I had depended on myself and my faith to get through my hard times. For more than ten years, I hadn't trusted other people to stand with me. And if I'd gotten back my medical license before being asked to give up my seat on the plane, I don't know how that would have changed what I did next, but the fact is that I was more optimistic about my future in June 2017 than I'd been in a long time.

The next complication in the process of regaining my medical license came almost immediately. The Kentucky Medical Board informed me that, despite my having passed my CPEP evaluation, they were still going to place restrictions on my medical license. First, I would need to report to a preceptor every two weeks. Second, I would not be allowed to practice medicine on my own and could only work as part of a group practice. The fact that I had practiced medicine for decades, including recently in Vietnam, and had recently passed my skills evaluation didn't seem to change anyone's opinion. It also didn't seem to matter that plenty of physicians still practiced at age seventy. While I was technically allowed to practice medicine with these two restrictions in place, the fact was that either restriction effectively barred me from practicing.

Requiring that I continue to check in with a preceptor ended my practice before it began for the simple reason that I could no longer find a preceptor. My previous preceptor, Dr. Godfrey, had informed me that he was retiring from his practice and could no longer act as a preceptor for me. This put me back in the same situation I'd been in two years earlier, when I couldn't find anyone willing to act as a preceptor for a returning physician with a criminal record.

Also, there was the requirement that I was only allowed to work within a group practice. This didn't work for the same reason that I couldn't find a preceptor. Most doctors didn't want to work with a man who had a criminal record. On top of that, there was more than a little prejudice against me for being seventy years old; no doubt many doctors would assume that my medical knowledge would be outdated, especially given the fact that I hadn't practiced in the United States for more than a decade. Furthermore, the fact that I had a restricted license made me look like a bad risk. Essentially, I had to join a group practice because of my restricted license, but group practices didn't want to take me on because of the restricted license.

Yet another problem prevented me from finding a preceptor or a group practice that would work with me. Six months earlier, there might have been a chance that any potential patient I saw would know about my past criminal conviction. But the conviction was from more than a decade earlier, and only people conducting background checks on me would likely find out about it. After what had happened with United Airlines, however, there was no place in the United States I could practice without people knowing that I was that guy from the airplane video. Even though I had done nothing wrong, most doctors were not eager to be connected with the kind of celebrity status I'd earned.

To give you a better idea of why a group practice wouldn't want to have me working with them, imagine that one of the other doctors in the practice was involved in a malpractice suit. It's the sort of thing that happens quite frequently, even though many times the doctor has not done anything wrong. Since these suits are so common, they're rarely reported as news. And since they're often quietly settled, they have no long-term effect on a doctor's or a practice's reputation. On the other hand, if a malpractice suit is brought against a practice *and* the man who got dragged off a United Airlines flight is involved, suddenly there's a stronger chance that the news media will cover the story. Even if I wasn't directly involved in such a suit, headlines like "United Victim Involved in Malpractice Suit" would likely run on websites and in newspapers, prompting people to read further. My case had already been proven to generate web traffic, so it would make sense for news media to connect it to an otherwise routine story in order to attract interest. Therefore, not hiring me would be the easiest way for a practice to avoid that sort of potential boost in unwanted media attention. It wasn't fair, but it was understandable.

Any mistake I made, or even the appearance of any mistake, would bring an extreme amount of media attention. People had been supportive of me during the month after the incident on the airplane, but I couldn't count on that goodwill to last. Negative stories about my past had circulated as well. While United Airlines wouldn't post any negative stories about me, none of the news media organizations on the planet had signed that settlement agreement. Any negative article about me would be sure to generate web traffic, whether or not it was accurate, and clearly I was going to be under that level of scrutiny for the rest of my life.

But the simple fact was that I still enjoyed practicing medicine. I still wanted to use everything I'd learned to help people. And if I couldn't find a preceptor or a group practice willing to work with me to do it, then I needed to have those restrictions lifted from my medical license. Frankly, it was ridiculous that after years of taking tests, filling out forms, and meeting unreasonable demands of every sort, I should still be struggling just to build a basic practice.

When I spoke with Clay Wortham about what had happened, he agreed that I had the basis for a lawsuit against the Kentucky Medical Board. The restrictions that they'd placed on my medical license were unreasonable. I had gone through an excessive number of tests, and I had more than earned the right to practice medicine again without restriction. Clay suggested that my conviction in 2005 might have unfairly prejudiced members of the board against me. Unfortunately, Clay was moving to Chicago and wouldn't be able to represent me; when I reached out to his firm, they refused to take my case.

Clay recommended a different law firm that would be willing to take it on. Unfortunately, there are problems with such a suit. In many ways, they're the same problems that I would have faced with an extended lawsuit against United Airlines. A lawsuit against the Kentucky Medical Board could take years, it would cost a lot of money that I likely wouldn't get back, and I had no guarantee of winning. I had other things I wanted to do with my life, and, as always, any decision I made would also affect my family.

But at this time, I'm still considering my options.

Chapter Thirty-Six

I've mentioned how I want to help immigrants, veterans, and people too poor to afford basic necessities such as medical care. I don't want to boast about this desire, as if it makes me an exceptional person. I simply have a skill set and the resources necessary to provide help. I truly believe that most people want to help those less fortunate; it's just that many of us don't know where to begin.

This belief in the innate goodness of other people was reaffirmed, ironically enough, shortly after what happened to me on the United Airlines flight. While getting beaten and dragged off an airplane might have left me feeling bitter about my fellow man, instead I was overwhelmed by an outpouring of sympathy from around the world. People saw the video of what happened to me and wanted to help. Not knowing any other way to help, they chose to share the video with as many people as they could, making certain that what happened to me couldn't be ignored. They also contacted both representatives at United Airlines and their elected officials to voice their disapproval. People armed with nothing but telephones and social media accounts forced changes to be made.

The support didn't last. Once I reached a settlement with United Airlines, I began seeing other comments being posted. The assumption was that I had settled for a massive amount of money and that I was now wealthy. And once people thought that I had become wealthy because of my settlement, some of them began to wonder if I had somehow exaggerated what had happened in order to get that money.

While I'm not allowed to divulge the amount of money I received, if anyone considers me wealthy, then it's because of what Teresa and I earned from our medical practices, what I earned through my property investments, and my earnings as a professional poker player. If I'm wealthy, then I was wealthy before this incident happened and I'm wealthy because I worked for it.

Another unexpected result of the settlement was that, on the assumption I was newly wealthy, people began reaching out to me for donations. Never mind the medical expenses I'd incurred during my recovery—I'd lost two teeth, had to have reconstructive surgery on my nose, and needed medication to deal with my headaches—and never mind the fact that group practices were unwilling to take me on as a partner, resulting in a loss of potential earnings. I began receiving phone calls and email messages asking me to share the money from a settlement that most people imagined to be much larger than it was. As I had at first done with news reporters after the incident, I began to withdraw and isolate myself from the public rather than address all these requests.

Maybe worst of all were the people who assumed that, because I had so much money, I could now retire. Coming from strangers, this was understandable, but it made me sad to hear this from family and friends. I had spent years trying to get my medical license back and invested tens of thousands of dollars in the process. All the while, I was earning income from several other sources. I hadn't needed a medical practice to pay my bills in over a decade. How could anyone who'd known me for years truly believe that I just wanted my medical practice back for the money? I wanted my medical practice back because I wanted to practice medicine.

If I retired, I would need to find something else to do to occupy my time. And there was nothing I wanted to do other than practice medicine again. If I was able to set up the veterans' clinic as I hoped, there was a good chance that I would never make any money with it; so perhaps I was retiring from running a profit-making medical practice. Really, I'd retired from that business more than ten years before that point. But even if it had been a sort of retirement (albeit not by choice), I was still going to practice medicine once more.

Unfortunately, nothing about my settlement with United Airlines fixed the problems I was having with the Kentucky Medical Board. So there I was, sitting at home, watching television once again. I suppose I could have spent my time then feeling sorry for myself, but that wouldn't have helped anyone. I had time and money. My health was improving with every day of rest. Whatever was happening with my medical license, I still had all the skills I'd learned in medical school. And besides all of that, I now had one other thing thanks to the incident: notoriety. If I had something to say, the media would cover it simply because of what had happened to me.

The question was, *What should I say?* I was already making plans to write a book, but there had to be more that I could talk about than just myself. Who else could benefit from the attention that my new celebrity status gave to me? If I showed myself in public, the media would take notice, so why not go somewhere that the media should be covering anyway?

I was still thinking about how best to direct the media attention that would inevitably focus on me in August 2017. That's when Hurricane Harvey reached the mainland United States, devastating Houston, Texas. Sitting in my home in Kentucky, I spent several days watching the disaster unfold through television coverage. I also watched as relief efforts began for the people who had survived. I knew that I could find at least one Houston-based organization that could use a donation. But I wanted to do more. I could do a lot more than just write a check.

As it happened, I didn't have to spend any time searching for an organization. The Viet Love Foundation reached out to me about participating in a benefit concert they were planning. This was a nonprofit organization that provided aid to Vietnamese communities hit by natural disasters. In times of crisis, some people get help faster than others. Some people get more help than others as well. And the people who have to wait the longest for basic things like food, shelter, and medicine tend to be minorities. I'd certainly heard about the varying responses that people got when asking for government aid, depending on whether they were of European, Asian, African, or Middle Eastern ancestry, for example. I knew that organizations like the Viet Love Foundation were necessary. I also knew they needed all the help they could get.

I had more than a little experience raising money and awareness for Vietnamese refugees in the past. I'm sure that the people connected with Viet Love knew about the benefit concert I'd organized in Seattle decades earlier. They might have heard about the two fund-raising concerts I'd organized in 2015 to raise money for a Buddhist temple in Kentucky. They might even have known about the intensive care unit I'd set up back in Vietnam a few years earlier.

But I'm positive that they contacted me primarily because of what had happened on the United Airlines flight. While I was a minor celebrity to the general public, I was especially well-known in the Vietnamese community. The assault I'd suffered mirrored the experiences that too many Vietnamese people still have in this country. The fact that I hadn't made any public appearances or statements since the incident would make my appearance at the benefit concert an even bigger draw for the media.

I suppose I could have just shown up at the event and said something to the crowd. But I was a musician. And it had been years since I'd performed anywhere. I agreed to attend, and I agreed to sing. I even wrote a new song especially for the event.

People around the world had offered their support to me after what had happened. But the Vietnamese community in particular had been extremely supportive. People had written thousands of comments on social media platforms, as well as sent emails and made phone calls to people in authority on my behalf. I will never know the names of everyone who took the time to express their outrage, and even if I did, it would have been impossible to contact all of them. But this benefit concert, meant to help many of the people who had helped me not so long before…this was a way that I could offer my thanks to them. I might not ever get another chance like this.

Although the benefit concert was intended to help the Vietnamese community in Houston, part of it was being held in Westminster, California, in Orange County. I was going to this event alone, since my wife couldn't take time away from her practice. And I was still recovering from my concussion, which meant that I wasn't going to drive myself from Kentucky to California, then from California to Texas. That meant I needed to get back on an airplane.

I was nervous about getting back on an airplane, but that wasn't the only problem. I was also nervous about making a public appearance after four months of isolating myself. My attorney wouldn't have recommended doing this…which is probably why I didn't bother to tell him about it. My wife was worried about my going to the concert as well; besides concerns over my slow recovery, she was also worried because I was literally walking into a disaster area.

Once I got there, the people at Viet Love treated me well and helped me through the whole process. The concert ran from three to ten o'clock, and most of the performing artists were Vietnamese. I performed my song, "Survive the Hurricane," at nine thirty, near the end. While we performed to a large audience, there was also a webcast of the entire event. The webcast was what pulled in the bulk of the donations; I thought I could do something to help get one final burst of donations from people watching at the end of the night. So I offered to match any donations made between the time I sang my song and the end of the event. That provided only a small window of thirty minutes, but I later found out that in that time alone we managed to raise $160,000.

Returning to Kentucky, Teresa was happy that the event had gone well and that nothing had befallen me, although I could tell that she was a bit surprised to discover that I'd donated $160,000 to the benefit group. But what good was the money doing me otherwise? I was no closer to getting my clinic started. And besides, part of the reason I'd received any cash settlement at all was because of all the outcry from other people, so why shouldn't I share the money? It wasn't like a hurricane could pay out cash settlements to the people whose houses it had destroyed.

A few weeks after the concert, I returned to Houston to see how the recovery efforts were going. One of the things that we tend to forget is that while the media soon loses interest in a disaster, the people affected by it are still trying to recover. By September of 2017, I'm sure a lot of people had forgotten about Hurricane Harvey, just as I knew that many of them had forgotten about the United Airlines incident.

After more than a month, I saw that many people were still waiting for basic aid. Despite their best efforts, the Red Cross, FEMA, and other organizations had been unable to help every community affected. It wasn't just people needing new houses, there were still people who lacked food and clean water. I'm sure it's difficult for many people in the United States to imagine that the basic needs of people in their own country may be left unmet, but the fact is that no amount of planning can cover everyone affected by a natural disaster as large as such a hurricane.

When I returned to Kentucky, I still hadn't made any progress in restarting my own medical practice. I hadn't yet decided whether to file a lawsuit against the Kentucky Medical Board, and I still didn't know what I wanted to do next. I was seventy years old, and despite the time and money available to me, I felt as if my options were limited. At that point, I began working on my book.

At the start of 2018, my medical career was still on hold, but I'd found other opportunities to help people. While other Vietnamese communities in the United States could use help, I couldn't forget the support I'd received from people living in Vietnam. I already had firsthand experience with the troubles people faced in my home country, so in February, I made another visit.

While I spent some time catching up with my brother, the bulk of my time was spent trying to provide assistance to various people in the area. My first stop was a small village between Vietnam and Cambodia. About two hundred poverty-stricken families in this village needed help. I next visited a village in Kontum that had a population somewhere between fifty and a hundred people, most of whom were either orphans from neighboring villages or the nuns who cared for them. These small communities lacked the resources to care for these parentless children, so it fell to various Lutheran and Catholic charities to supply them with the food and medicine they needed. After that, I visited three more orphan villages, all with the same problems and all needing so much more help than I could provide.

Unlike the benefit concert in Texas, I decided to visit the first village with a minimum of media exposure. Besides my immediate family, nobody knew I was going. This wasn't about raising awareness so much as just reaching out and helping people. Once I got there, I found that I couldn't help nearly as much as I'd hoped. I was told that I would not be receiving government approval to practice medicine in the village, so my help would be restricted to handing out food and helping with basic maintenance there. I was never told why I wasn't allowed to practice medicine in the village, but by that point I'd grown used to unreasonable restrictions. Besides offering basic help to that village and two others, I was also able to offer donations of money to the nuns so they could continue with their work, including being able to repair a number of broken beds in the orphanages I saw.

Once again, Teresa was unable to join me. And once again, she was worried about me. This time, however, she was worried about more than just my health. Rumors were circulating about the amount of money I'd received from my settlement with United Airlines, and anyone doing basic research on me would have found out about the donation I'd made to the Viet Love Foundation. Teresa was concerned that my notoriety and the fact that people assumed I was wealthy would make me a target for kidnapping. We'd both heard stories about wealthy travelers being abducted for ransoms.

But I tried not to worry about it. There had been no media coverage of my trip. Besides that, I had faith that, as long as I was trying to help people, I would be all right. I was involved in an auto accident in the highland of Ban Me Thuot, but nobody got hurt. Otherwise, I experienced no trouble during the trip. I leave it up to others to decide if my faith was well-founded, but I believe that someone above was watching over me.

While I was visiting the orphan villages, I was told about another village in the Central Highlands—Pleiku was populated exclusively by lepers. Most of the local communities lacked the resources to care for these individuals, so they were all isolated in one place and left to depend on Christian organizations and donations to survive. The priest in charge of their care hired nurses to tend their skin lesions. I gave funds for the lepers to be able to buy food as well as donating an amount sufficient to keep the place going for three months. Honestly, I could have spent the rest of my life visiting one village after another, finding more people who needed my help.

But there was only so much I could do. The Vietnamese government wouldn't let me practice medicine, and the nuns were handling the day-to-day tasks just fine. All I could really do to help was to give money…and I could do that from Kentucky.

I went back to my family and began planning the next stage of my life.

Chapter Thirty-Seven

While I was dealing with my restricted medical license and planning for the benefit concert in Texas, the airlines were still dealing with backlash from the April incident. While many reporters were calling this an isolated incident and stressing that what happened to me wasn't representative of a typical flying experience, the fact was that a lot of people could relate to what had happened to me.

None of the people voicing their complaints had been dragged off an airplane and treated so roughly that they'd needed to be hospitalized. But they could certainly relate to being treated with disrespect by airline staff. What had happened to me had been done in front of a plane filled with passengers, with several of them pointing their smartphones at the security team to record everything. The security personnel clearly saw nothing wrong with what they were doing, since they had no problem being recorded while doing it. And, whether they intended it that way or not, physically assaulting a passenger in front of other passengers creates an unspoken threat that the same thing could happen to anyone who voices an objection.

Even the people who voiced their support for United Airlines ended up highlighting the problem. By stating that United had the right to treat me in this fashion, it was implied that United (and any other airline by extension) had the right to treat any other passenger the same way. The debate had begun to devolve into the question of whether passengers deserved to be treated like paying customers or like unruly prisoners. The effect of this debate was that many potential passengers were opting not to fly on United flights so as not to run the same risk.

But yet another backlash forced the government to get involved. People weren't only worried about how they would be treated on United Airlines flights. They were concerned about how they would be treated on *any* airplane or airline in the United States. Since the news coverage of the incident frequently mentioned the intervention of local police, the impression (especially in other countries) was that this was indicative of how people were treated in the United States. Again, it didn't help United or the airline industry in general that the man who'd been assaulted on camera had been Asian.

Shortly after the incident, representatives of United Airlines appeared before Congress to answer questions about what had happened as well as what they planned to do to make sure this sort of episode never happened again. The US Department of Transportation was also investigating the incident. While I wasn't asked to appear either time, my attorney did receive updates. The results of the hearing and the investigation could probably be considered a mixed bag.

First, the US Department of Transportation determined that, while United Airlines had made a mistake in how they removed me from the plane, there was no evidence that I'd been singled out because of my ethnicity. Furthermore, what happened to me was deemed to be a single isolated incident. Since the Department of Transportation was only authorized to act to address patterns of illegal activity, no official action would be taken against United for this one incident. I never found out how many passengers needed to be physically assaulted before it could be considered a pattern.

To be fair, while the legal consequences left something to be desired, the airline industry itself took several positive steps toward making sure this sort of confrontation didn't happen again. The CEO of United Airlines, Oscar Munoz, issued multiple apologies, along with assurances. The Chicago Department of Aviation followed through on this promise with several simple changes.

I'm sure that many of the passengers failed to intervene on my behalf because they thought the Chicago Police Department was arresting me for some reason. It was a reasonable assumption, since the word *police* appeared prominently on the security guards' uniforms. But the security guards who dragged me off of that plane were not police officers and did not have any of the legal authority of police officers. So the first positive change was to simply remove the word *police* from their uniforms.

The Chicago Department of Aviation issued a statement that not only condemned the actions of the security team, but also acknowledged that security guards should never have even been on that plane in the first place. Questions about overbooking were classified as customer service issues, and there was no reason that a security guard needed to be called for a customer service issue. The revised rules would make clear that security teams would only be called to board a plane if there was either an immediate medical issue or an imminent physical threat.

And that brought us to the fact that passengers could be removed from flights they'd paid for in the first place. While it might surprise a lot of people, ending this practice was never even considered. Flying an airplane is very expensive. The runways need to be maintained, the planes need to be maintained, the staff needs to be paid, and the fuel is expensive. No airline could afford to fly half-filled planes for long without either raising fares significantly or going out of business. That's why many flights are oversold—to compensate for last-minute cancellations.

However, just because passengers could still get bumped from their flights didn't mean there wasn't plenty of room for improvement. First, the compensation that could be offered to passengers who voluntarily left the plane was brought up to ten thousand dollars. Passengers could no longer be removed once they'd been seated on the plane. Crewmembers making last-minute must-ride bookings now had to make those bookings no later than sixty minutes before departure (as opposed to being able to make such bookings right up to the moment of departure). Finally, not as many flights would be overbooked.

While all these changes make sense to me, I don't believe that what happened to me was because of a poorly written guideline. Rather, it was a matter of respect. It was the assumption that people didn't deserve dignity unless they could afford to bring legal action against someone. And while various individuals involved in this incident promised that passenger dignity would be maintained, I couldn't help but feel that the change needed wouldn't be accomplished simply by issuing new guidelines.

Chapter Thirty-Eight

My story hasn't ended yet. It's been more than a year since the United Airlines incident, and the airline industry is still implementing changes. It's been more than ten years since I was arrested and forced to give up my medical license, and I'm still fighting to have that license reinstated without restriction. It's been more than thirty years since I first met my wife, and our relationship has continued to grow as we've raised five children and watched them leave one by one to build their own lives. It's been more than forty years since I first arrived in the United States, and I'm still fighting against the same prejudice that Vietnamese refugees (and other immigrants) have always had to endure.

While I was making my plans to visit Vietnam in February of 2018, Teresa retired from her pediatric practice. I'm sure that many people believe I should stop trying to get my license fully reinstated so my wife and I can just enjoy our retirement together. But the fact is that neither of us is ready to fully stop working. So while I try to get the restrictions taken off my medical license, Teresa is pursuing new interests she never had the time to explore while practicing medicine. And we each support the other in those decisions.

When I returned from Vietnam once more, I began spending more time with my wife and children. One unexpected benefit of the United Airlines incident was that it ended up bringing our family closer together than we'd been since my arrest years earlier. As of 2018, Crystal had dropped out of law school in order to raise her three children; Christine was a professor of medicine at the University of North Carolina; both Ben and his wife still practiced internal medicine in Syracuse, New York; Angela was still working through her OB/GYN residency in Cleveland; and Timothy was still a cardiologist in Dallas, Texas. Throughout all my struggles, I somehow managed to raise five children who all make me proud. And now that several of them have children of their own, Teresa and I have plenty of grandchildren to dote on as we take every opportunity to travel across the country.

Even a year after the United Airlines incident, I still need to be careful not to draw too much attention to myself. Since that incident, there have been hundreds of major news stories generating multitudes of new accidental celebrities, so most people have long forgotten my name. But every time any airline gets involved in a scandal of any kind, some reporter will invariably bring up the fact that the airline industry has seen its share of scandals in recent years, including what happened to me. The truth is that I'm never quite sure when my name will reappear in the news.

I still want to open a clinic to help treat veterans and poor people. I will never forget how I first arrived in this country with nothing and how soldiers and church groups offered me help with no expectation of ever being repaid for their efforts. I hate seeing so many of these veterans falling on hard times now, in need of the same help they offered so freely to me and so many others years ago. While I came to this country after the fall of Saigon, there will always be governments that are falling apart. And there will always be refugees coming to this country with nothing but hope. I want to help the men and women who helped me when I was an immigrant, as well as help the immigrants who are arriving here today with nothing more than I had when I first arrived here.

When I was singled out on that United Airlines flight, I'm sure that no one but my wife knew what I had gone through in my life. I risked dying on the Pacific Ocean to reach this country. I not only worked in a prison but was physically attacked by one of the inmates. I ran marathons. I faced off against some of the finest poker players in the world. I spent more than a decade fighting various bureaucracies in order to get my medical license reinstated. I raised five children. Had the airport personnel known all of that ahead of time, would they still have assumed that I would be easy to intimidate?

Maybe they would have. But my story is far from unique. Millions of refugees have arrived in this country over the years under conditions as bad or even worse than the privations and dangers I endured on my way to the US. Immigrants still routinely face discrimination when attending school, applying for jobs, or just sitting on an airplane. The legal system is designed so that it is still far too easy for an innocent man to lose his profession and even his freedom due to a false accusation.

And for all I knew, my wife and I might not have been the only immigrants on board. We might not have even been the only refugees from Vietnam on that plane. There might have been someone else who'd lost his or her career due to a false accusation. There most certainly were other people who'd had to start their lives over again after an unexpected setback, as well as people who'd dealt with the challenges of raising children. And I'm certain there were other people aboard who'd weathered challenges that I would find unimaginable. And every last one of them deserved to be treated with dignity.

I did not tell my story so that people would feel sorry for me. When all of the good and bad of my life is measured, I have been very fortunate. I met my wife by an unexpected coincidence. Losing my medical license led to my discovering a faith in God, as well as pursuing various other interests that I never would have explored if I'd been running a medical practice all that time. The incident on the airplane led to a truly overwhelming amount of support from people all over the world. And despite the many setbacks I've suffered, I am now in a position to help far more people than I ever could have if I'd maintained my medical practice without interruption.

I want you to know that, whoever you are, right now you are part of a story similar to my own. Maybe you have to deal with prejudice because of your race, your gender, your age, your religion, or your sexual orientation. Or maybe you are in a position to help someone dealing with such prejudice. Or maybe you are one of those who believes that one person or another doesn't deserve respect for any of those reasons. Whoever you are in that story, you can make it better simply by remembering that we all deserve to be treated with dignity. Money can give us the power to discriminate, but it never gives us the right to do so. And the easiest way to fight against any prejudice is to call it out when you see it.

You won't always win those fights, but you will never be ashamed that you fought them. Never give up, and always have faith.

About the Author

Dr. David Dao immigrated to the United States in 1975 as a refugee from the Vietnam War. He and his wife, Teresa, are both physicians, and they have five grown children—four doctors and one attorney.

Born in Vietnam, he now lives in Elizabethtown, Kentucky.

Mango Publishing, established in 2014, publishes an eclectic list of books by diverse authors—both new and established voices—on topics ranging from business, personal growth, women's empowerment, LGBTQ studies, health, and spirituality to history, popular culture, time management, decluttering, lifestyle, mental wellness, aging, and sustainable living. We were recently named 2019 *and* 2020's #1 fastest growing independent publisher by *Publishers Weekly.* Our success is driven by our main goal, which is to publish high quality books that will entertain readers as well as make a positive difference in their lives.

Our readers are our most important resource; we value your input, suggestions, and ideas. We'd love to hear from you—after all, we are publishing books for you!

Please stay in touch with us and follow us at:
Facebook: Mango Publishing
Twitter: @MangoPublishing
Instagram: @MangoPublishing
LinkedIn: Mango Publishing
Pinterest: Mango Publishing
Newsletter: mangopublishinggroup.com/newsletter

Join us on Mango's journey to reinvent publishing, one book at a time.